Around Historic Lancashire
written and illustrated by David Jessop

Morris Men in Garstang celebrating Easter

MIDAS BOOKS

Acknowledgements

I would like to thank all the people who have helped to make this book possible. Many of whom I have not met, but they have given their time and knowledge freely. Also the National Trust, the Civic Trust for the North West, and their various associations. Not forgetting my family and friends for all their help and encouragement.

Many of the houses illustrated are private residences. Anyone wishing to visit should either check first or respect other people's privacy, and simply look from a respectable distance and move on, for there are lots more to see elsewhere.

Houses and museums which are open to the public often have restricted access, and their opening times can be obtained from either the nearest Tourist Information Centre or direct from the North West Tourist Board.

D.J.

In the same illustrated series
Around the Historic Chilterns by Ron Pigram
Around Historic Devon and Cornwall by Desmond Post and Stuart Richmond
Around Historic Hampshire by Colin Wintle and Victor Spink
Around Historic Kent by Malcolm John and C.A.T. Brigden
Around Historic Somerset and Avon by Colin Wintle and Nicola Luscombe
Around Historic Sussex by Ray Miller and Gerald Lip
Around Historic Yorkshire by Jeffrey Lee and Les Coldrick

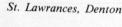 First Published 1978 by
MIDAS BOOKS
12 Dene Way, Speldhurst,
Tunbridge Wells, Kent TN3 0NX

© David Jessop 1978

Typeset and artwork by VDU Characters, Edenbridge, Kent.
Printed in Great Britain by Billing & Sons Ltd, Guildford, London and Worcester.

ISBN O 85936 108 X
Price: £3.25 net.

St. Lawrances, Denton

Contents and Illustrations

Roman parade helmet found at Ribchester.

Aldingham	6
Arkholme	7
Astley Hall	8
Birkrigg Common	9
Blackstone Edge	10
Bolton-by-Bowland	11
Bolton-le-Sands	12
Borwick Hall	13
Bretherton, Carr House	14
Broughton	15
Caldervale	16
Cartmel Priory Church	17
Cartmel Priory Gatehouse	18
Caton	19
Chipping	20
Clitheroe	21
Cockersand Abbey	22
Colne	23
Conishead Priory	24
Coniston, Brantwood	25
Cowan Bridge	26
Croston	27
Croxteth Hall	28
Downham	29
Eccleston	30
Edisford Bridge	31
Fairfield, Moravian Settlement	32
Fleetwood, Rossall School	33
Foxdenton Hall	34
Furness Abbey	35
Gawthorpe Hall	36
Gisburn	37
Glasson Dock	38
Goosenargh, Chingle Hall	39
Hackensall Hall	40
Haigh Hall	41
Hall-i-th-wood, Bolton	42
Halton	43
Hawkshead	44
Hawkshead Courthouse	45
Heaton Hall	46

Hesketh Bank	47
Hest Bank	48
Heysham, St. Peter's/St. Patrick's	49
Higher Mill Museum, Rossendale	50
Hoghton Tower	51
Holker Hall	52
Hornby	53
Hornby, St. Margaret's Church	54
Hurstwood	55
Kersall Cell	56
Knowsley Hall	57
Lancaster, Castle	58
Lancaster Castle, Shire Hall	59
Lancaster, Friends Meetinghouse	60
Lancaster, Priory Church St. Mary	61
Lancaster, St. Georges Quay	62, 63
Map of Lancashire	64, 65
Lancaster, Town Cross/Judges Lodgings	66
Lathom Park Chapel	67
Leighton Hall	68
Liverpool	69
Lower Hodder Bridges	70
Mains Hall	71
Manchester, Cathedral	72
Manchester, Castlefield	73
Manchester, Cheethams	74
Manchester, Free Trade Hall	75
Manchester, Liverpool Road Station	76
Manchester, Old Wellington Inn	77
Manchester, The Portico Library	78
Manchester, St. Annes Church	79
Manchester, St. John's Street	80
Mawdesley	81
Middleton	82
Mitton	83
Newchurch-in-Pendle	84
Newton	85
Ordsall Hall	86
Overton/Sunderland Point	87
Piel Castle	88
Pilling	89
Platt Hall	90
Preston	91
Preston, Walton Bridge	92
Radcliffe Tower	93
Rawcliffe Hall	94
Ribchester	95
Ribchester, White Bull Inn	96
Rivington	97
Rochdale, Pioneers	98
Rossendale, Higher Mill Museum	50
Roughlee Hall	99
Rufford Old Hall	100
Samlesbury Church	101
Samlesbury Hall	102
Sawley Abbey	103
Scarisbrick Hall	104
Sefton	105
Slaidburn	106
Smithill's Hall	107
Southport	108
Speke Hall	109
Stonyhurst College	110
Swarthmoor Hall	111
Thornton, Marsh Mill	112
Towneley Hall	113
Turton Stone Circle	114
Turton Tower	115
Ulverston	116
Urswick	117
Warrington	118
Warton	119
Whalley Abbey	120
Whalley Church	121
Wigan	122
Worsley, Bridgewater Canal	123
Wrea Green	124
Wray	125
Wycoller	126
Wythenshawe Hall	127
Yealand Conyers	128

Foreword

Grimy hunched warehouses hanging over canals that smell positively mauve: Stooped old ladies with clogs and shawls, clattering towards grey mills . . . Skyline leaden and darkened with belching chimneys: Rain swept streets, huddling together gazing eyeless onto cobbled thoroughfares . . . Images of Lancashire conjured up in the minds of most people who live South of Watford Gap. How can words paint the sweep of the Trough of Bowland? The bustle of Liverpool and the cosmopolitan energy of Manchester cannot be thrown onto the canvas of mere prose, nor can the aged stones of Clitheroe be conveyed in print. The brooding Pennines that have borne mute testimony to the clash of the Houses of Lancaster and York: The broad canopy of Kirby Lonsdale towards the Lakes, the Lancashire of sweet moorland air the county of greatness.

Les Dawson

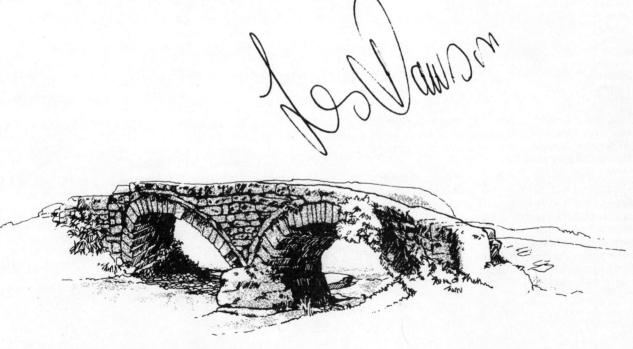

Aldingham

Following the coast road from Ulverston, passing Conishead Priory and Birkrigg Common, we come across a sign marked 'Aldingham', directing us to one of the most interesting churches of Low Furness.

On a warm sunny day there is no better place than Aldingham for children to collect stones and sea shells, but the old church knows well the fury and winds of the sea. So close is it to the sea that high tides wash the churchyard walls and sea water sprays the grass. It is said that long ago tidal waves swept away half of Aldingham.

The ancient church is believed to have been one of the resting places for the body of St Cuthbert on its last journey.

More recent visitors have included Durham miners, convalescing at Conishead Priory.

Returning to the coast road, and heading south, there is a hill known as 'The Moat' where once stood the Norman Castle of Le Flemings. Inland and sheltered from the ravages of the sea, are the ruins of Gleaston Castle, built by the Harringtons as part of their defence against the Scots.

Arkholme

The 'airdh' or shieling of the Norsemen down by the Lune levels, this village was known as Aaram in olden times.

Since the time of Ulf and the Domesday survey the land has been owned by the Lords of Hornby. It was part of the Lordship of Melling, a rich parish so vast that it was divided into 'quarterings'. Part of the Arkholme-cum-Cawood chapelry was separated from Melling by the river, which meant that for festivals and burials local folk had to cross by Wenning ferry and walk to Melling church, often at risk to their lives because of frequent flooding.

Arkholme is one of those 'long' country villages, following the line of an old lane which quietly wends its way from the main Halton-Kirby highway, down the side of the valley to the old ford across the river Lune. This is a true village with no two houses alike, many with carved dates and names. The inhabitants are rightly proud of this obvious contender in the Best Kept Village Competition and there is no better place to enjoy the beautiful Lonsdale landscape.

Down towards the river the church is built on the hillside, on a site of twelfth century Motte and Baily castle.

Astley Hall

Set in its own beautiful parkland, Astley once belonged to the
Knights Hospitallers of St John of Jerusalem. It was their
tenants, the Charnocks, who built a half-timbered two-storeyed
Tudor house, the remains of which can still be seen.

Robert Charnock was a Royalist; a king's man through and
through, though his loyalty during the Civil Wars cost him dear. When he
died in 1653, his daughter inherited the estate and married the son of Sir
Peter Brooke of Mere in Cheshire.

In the 1660s the front of the house was extensively rebuilt in early
Jacobean style, gaining an extra floor at the same time. It was also adorned
with carvings, portraits and some of the finest plaster ceilings to be seen
anywhere. In the Long Gallery can be found a 23$\frac{1}{2}$ft long shovelboard —
one of the longest surviving examples of the game.

The estate passed from the Brookes to the Parkers and, through them, to
Reginald Arthur Tatton, who gave Astley to the township in 1922.

Astley Park has become part of the 'Central Lancashire Development' —
a new town 'village', while the Hall contains collections of furniture,
paintings and pottery.

Birkrigg Common

On a fine clear summer's afternoon, with the wind fresh in my face and the sun burning the ground, I wandered over Birkrigg Common in search of an ancient circle of stones.

The view was magnificent. All around was blue and green and gold. Morecambe Way was shimmering in the haze. There were the woods of far off Holker Hall, with Cartmel Priory beyond. Conishead Priory was set like a jewel amidst the trees, clear and bright in the afternoon sun. Surveying all was Ulverston's lighthouse set against the heart of Lakeland's mountains — a fitting monument to the town's distinguished son, John Barrow.

Many things could have been seen from here through the centuries. Slave ships making their way to Greenodd, Quaker funeral processions to Sunbrick Sepulchre, iron ore trundled down to Bardsea until the lanes were red — even the Romans came here in search of precious iron — ships laden with slate, pig iron, charcoal and gunpowder, while on the shore, shrimp carts followed the ebbing tide.

I walked down the hill, past Sunbrick and there, on the left, a few yards from the road, was the stone circle I had been looking for. Burial ground or Druid temple? Its past secrets safe in enduring stone.

Blackstone Edge

This old road on the Lancashire and Yorkshire border, is one of the early focal points for walkers starting out of Edale along the Pennine Way. Thought to be of Roman origin and holding many a mystery, its most curious feature is the central grove, or trough, running along its length, defying explanation.

This ancient track was certainly a pack horse route and was used by travellers over the Pennines until the eighteenth century. The descriptions by the seventeenth century diarist, Celia Fiennes, and Daniel Defoe in his *Tour Through England and Wales* would hardly encourage many people to visit Lancashire. Indeed, early travellers had daunting problems to contend with; flooding rivers, meres, bogs, and notoriously bad roads.

Blackstone Edge takes its name from the gritstone crags which rise to 1, 475ft. The top of the pass over the moor is marked by the 'Aiggin' stone; a wayside cross of medieval origin.

10

Bolton-by-Bowland

One of the loveliest villages to come into Lancashire in 1974, Bolton-by-Bowland has two village greens; one with the school and the old courthouse — now converted to a private dwelling; the lower green has the market cross and stocks, with a memorial garden, a stream and the church beyond.

The inn, butcher's shop, coffee house, and rows of seventeenth and eighteenth century houses complete the setting of this village.

The church contains the tomb of Sir Ralph Pudsey, the lid carved with portraits of the knight, his three wives, and his twenty-five sons and daughters. Henry VI was a guest of the Pudseys in 1464 while hiding from the Yorkists, and his whereabouts were kept secret for a year. Other notable features of the church are the font, the Bolton Hall Chapel and the fine carving on the pew doors.

The road to Gisburn crosses one of the most beautiful stretches of the Ribble. Here are the limestone cliffs where a Pudsey made his legendary leap; Arthur's Hole, the fairy-haunted cove; and where salmon spawn in November.

Bolton-le-Sands

Farming, sheep rearing on the salt marshes, and the gathering of cockles and mussels, were the occupations of Bolton-le-Sands inhabitants, but its position on the main highway to Scotland has caused its character and fortunes to change with the flow of traffic and time.

Recent developments have split the community, the old village of seventeenth century and Georgian houses, high on the hill; and the modern estate on the lower ground to the west, with the canal forming the dividing line.

The turnpike road of 1754 brought the postchaises, carriers' waggons, and flying machines (light horse-drawn vehicles that could make the journey from Kendal to London in three days), followed by the mail coaches.

On the bridge over the Kendal Canal, by the Packet Boat Inn, one may watch the pleasure boats making their progress and try to imagine the excitement of 1817, when the canal was completed, equalled only in the 1840s with the coming of the railways.

The petrol engine brought traffic jams to Bolton-le-Sands, later cured by a by-pass for the A6 and finally a motorway. Now the village has time to breathe, presenting a glimpse of times past.

Borwick Hall

In 1066, the estate of Borwick was part of Earl Tostig's lordship, and subsequently that of Roger of Poitou.

By 1499, the manor was held by Thomas Whittington who, it is thought, built the stone pele tower. The manor passed into the Redmayne family and, in 1567, part of the estate was bought by Richard Bindloss who, by the year 1590, had purchased the entire manor.

The Bindloss family were wealthy merchants of Kendal and it is to them that credit must go for the beautiful Elizabethan house, with its excellent example of a spinning gallery, that survives today.

The most colourful member of the Bindloss family was the wealthy and influential Sir Robert. The Civil War appears to have little effect on Sir Robert's fortunes, as he seems always to have been on the winning side. He was created a baronet by Charles I in 1641, and elected Member of Parliament for Lancaster, replacing a Royalist.

The future Charles II stayed at Borwick in 1631, on his way south prior to his defeat at Worcester. When Charles acquired the throne, Sir Robert was installed as Knight of the Shire, and was County Sheriff in 1671-73.

Borwick Hall is now a residential centre for young people, organised by the Lancashire Youth Clubs Association.

Bretherton, Carr House

We can easily recapture the past atmosphere of this countyside, with Will o' the Wisps and Jack o' Lanterns. Marshland of Christ's Croft, wild and lawless, a no-man's land for wanted men. The river Douglas busy with barges, and sea-going traffic all the way to Much Hoole and beyond.

On the western side of the Liverpool-Preston road there is a tollhouse. A turning leads to Bretherton and, on the left, stands Carr House, built by the Stone family in 1613, a rare feature of which is its cage-newel staircase.

The Stone family were traders from early Tudor times and with their fleet of sea-going ships they imported panel boards and oak from Ireland. It was the Stones who, in 1604, supplied timber to the Shuttleworths for the building of Gawthorpe Hall.

The remarkable church of Much Hoole is constructed of hand-made brick. Notable features are the many memorials to its one-time curate, Jeremiah Harocks. Born in Texteth, he was a self-taught astronomer and in 1639, at the age of 20, while lodging at Carr House, he accurately calculated the 'Transit of Venus' — a dark spot on the Sun's disc. In November of that year, witnessed by a friend, he recorded the event on makeshift equipment in the room above the porch.

14

Broughton

Each August, Broughton celebrates the granting of its market charter by Elizabeth I. It was an important town for the nearby Abbey of Furness. Important too, in its strategic position. The tower overlooking the town was built as part of a chain of defences against the Scottish raiders (see *Furness Abbey*).

The elegant Georgian square is packed with traffic in the summer months. It owes its existence to John Gilpin Sawrey, who came to live at the tower and commissioned a London architect to lay out the square which was built between 1760-66. The obelisk was erected by Sawrey's widow to mark the Jubilee of George III.

The Town Hall was originally the Market Hall. Note the Fish Stones once used for fixing the price of Duddon salmon, cockles and mussels.

Down the Duddon Estuary is the ancient church of Kirkby Ireleth, where the body of St Cuthbert is thought to have been carried in 875.

Caldervale

The development of the Lancashire textile industry did not happen by chance. Consistent rainfall in this part of the country meant that the streams from the water shed of the Pennines hardly ever ran dry. The early industrialists built their water-powered mills around the streams in the hills, resulting in industrial villages and hamlets spreading into the hills to the north. *(See Colne).*

The industry's dependence on water ended with the development of the steam engine and, by 1825, as many as 25 mills in Preston and 65 in Oldham were steam-powered, fuelled by Lancashire coal mines.

Steam changed the landscape, and red-brick and glass mills with their high chimneys dominated the skyline as well as the lives of their workers. Of the mills that have survived, few still weave and spin; most have lost both their chimneys and engines, and produce anything from spaghetti to foam rubber.

In 1835, the Jackson brothers planned and built the mill village of Caldervale on the banks of the Calder, bearing in mind the welfare of their workers as well as the interests of industry. A contrast to the horrors, squalor and waste in the back streets of the old cotton towns.

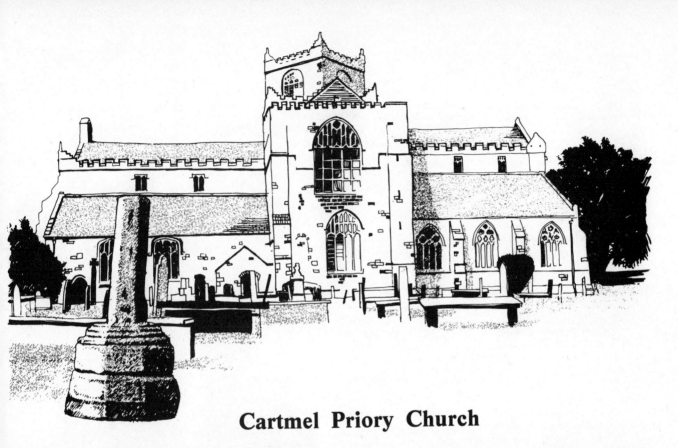

Cartmel Priory Church

In the year 1190, William Marshal, Earl of Pembroke, was granted licence to found a monastery for the Regular Canons of St Augustine. The situation, established by tradition, was between two rivers, one flowing north, the other south. Construction took the best part of a century, overtaxing the resources of the poor and thinly populated area.

Over the years, the prior entertained the great and noble, even Scottish Princes, in the hope of buying immunity from their raiding parties.

By the close of the fourteenth century the cloister buildings were settling badly in the unstable ground. The rebuilding was apparently more successful, as the new cloister, the diagonal belfry tower and the nave are thought to have survived from the fifteenth century.

Among the priory treasures is a first edition of Edmund Spenser's *Faerie Queene*.

In the churchyard can be seen the stump of a fifteenth century cross, and the tombstone of William Taylor, one of Willaim Wordworth's teachers.

17

Cartmel Priory Gatehouse

When the priory was dissolved in 1537, some of its canons joined the Pilgrimage of Grace and were executed in consequence. The whole of the priory was purchased for the use of the parish and gradually the buildings were demolished. Apart from the church, the only surviving building is the picturesque gatehouse, dating from about 1330. Standing in what is now the village square, the gatehouse was used as a grammar school from 1624 until 1790. It is now the property of the National Trust.

A small force of Roundhead soldiers arrived at Cartmel in October 1643, stabling their horses in the nave of the church. It is said that, angered by the impropriety of the act, some of the local men began shooting at the soldiers. The church door is traditionally known as 'Cromwell's Door' and during restoration work in 1955 fragments of lead were found embedded in the door. Another occasion when the peace of the village was disturbed was when George Fox preached there in 1653.

With the steady flow of 'oversands' visitors, trade increased and the village grew into one of the most beautiful in the country, justifying its regular awards in Best Kept Village Competitions.

Caton

Caton, close by the river
Lune, is a roadside village that has
grown with the times. The Romans
marked the site with their 5th milestone along the valley from
Lanchester, in whose Town Hall Museum it is now housed.

As defence against the raiding Scots, the owners of nearby
Gresgarth fortified their Hall by building a massive pele. This was part of the much
disputed border country and the people suffered greatly at the hands of the raiders,
especially during the terror of the Black Douglas in the fourteenth century.

The chance of revenge came when many a local man took arms and followed
Edward Stanley Hornby (later Lord Monteagle) on a march to the north that ended
in the victory of Flodden.

Caton still has its invaders, but they now come from the products of its artists and
craftsmen.

By the roadside, next to a brook, stands the remains of an oak tree. At its foot,
joined together by metal ties, are the 'fishstones'. It was here that the brethren from
Cockersand Abbey sold their surplus salmon.

Modern Caton spills into Brookhouse, whose prettiest aspect is enjoyed by the
view from the bridge, looking towards the church with the walk up Rotten Row by
the stream.

19

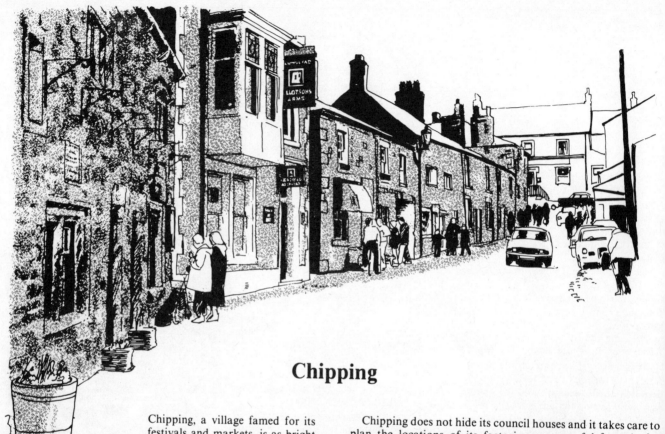

Chipping

Chipping, a village famed for its festivals and markets, is as bright and busy today as it has always been. Surrounded by some of the most beautiful countryside to be found anywhere, here is an ideal centre from which to explore Calder or Beacon fells.

Always a centre of industry: ironwork, chair-making, weaving and farming, the village once had as many as 5 mills driven by its brook. One of these mills is now restored and converted into a restaurant.

Chipping does not hide its council houses and it takes care to plan the locations of its factories; a successful formula for keeping a 'modern' village identity.

In the centre stands the church of St. Bartholomew with furniture and fittings displaying many of the villagers' skills.

On Windy Street stand John Brabbin's Grammar School and Alms houses, founded in the seventeenth century. John was the village lad who made good and, in his will, he left 20 guineas to establish a school in Newton. Next to the Post Office is Brabbin's birthplace; a cottage bearing a commemorative plaque.

Clitheroe

the Ribble Valley, on the 'old' border of Lancashire and orkshire, stands this ancient market town with a long and olourful history. Romans marched this way and after them the mies of the Normans, Scots, English, King and Cromwell.

The Norman castle of the De Laceys was built on the edge of a ile wide bed of limestone; the countryside, once part of the oyal Forest, is dotted with the remains of quarries, lime kilns, d the relics of spinning, weaving and bobbin industries.

Many of the Yorkshire villages further along the valley elonged to manors which made up the Honor of Clitheroe in orman times; when the county boundaries were redrawn in 974, it was no surprise to find these areas brought within the ew' county limits.

The twelfth century castle took quite a beating from Cromwell's men in 1649. Nevertheless, it is one of the most romantic landmarks of the area, providing a fine viewpoint of the valley; to the south east, the dark and mysterious Pendle Hill, Downham village, Bolton-by-Bowland and the Forest of Bowland; to the north, Easington and Waddington Fells; Longridge Fell is to the west, with Ribchester at its foot on the banks of the Ribble. No wonder the folk from these parts have always made for Clitheroe's markets and fairs.

21

Cockersand Abbey

Furness, Whalley and Cockersand are the only three establishments of religious orders to be found in Lancashire; a poor thinly populated land cannot support many large communities of devotion.

This remote, wild and windy spot, isolated by tides and marsh, was chosen by Hugh the Hermit as his cell. The Abbot of Leicester founded a hospital here for the sick and leprous, and an abbey was established around 1190.

In the fifteenth century Cockersand had its own quay for those who arrived by sea and its small lighthouse is thought to have been originated by the brethren.

The abbey provided rectors for Mitton All Hallows and Churchtown St. Helen's, which brought in revenues, but there were always financial difficulties, made worse by Scottish raiders, also the sea undermined the foundations. When the end came in Dissolution, much of the stonework was used for the building of local halls and farms. All that remains is the Chapter House, which shares a bleak and lonely shore-line with a solitary windswept tree.

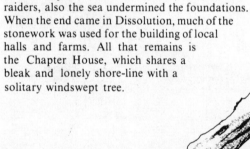

Colne

Overlooking the town to the south stand the earthworks of Castercliffe, an ancient Roman fort. The hills above Colne, Nelson and Burnley have more than their share of areas which are marked on maps as *tumuli* — earthworks of unknown origin.

The church dates back to a twelfth century chapel and was rebuilt in the early sixteenth century.

Astride an east-west highway, Colne has long been a market place for the hill folk, and the town's chief trade has always been the manufacture of cloth, weaving locally produced wool until well into the nineteenth century.

The textile industry was well established in the east of Lancashire from early Tudor times; a cottage industry, with each area specialising in the production of its own type of cloth.

Clothiers, mercers and drapers often organised the buying of the raw materials and the manufacturing processes, as well as the selling of the finished product. Small communities of hand-loom weavers developed, like those at Wyceller and Trawden, but collecting the cloth and transporting it to market was a risky business and highway robbery was rife.

Colne had its own Piece Hall, its two spacious rooms lined with booths where the merchants from London and York bought the cloth.

Conishead Priory

The priory was founded in the twelfth century on a site chosen by Augustinian monks, at first as a hospital for lepers and paupers although, over the years, it gradually became to be used solely as a priory.

When Henry VIII broke away from the Church of Rome, the monks were removed and the priory passed to the Crown.

Towards the end of the seventeenth century, ownership of the estate passed by marriage to the Braddyll family, in whose hands it remained for many years. When restoration was found necessary in 1821, Colonel Thomas Braddyll, decided instead to have the entire structure demolished and to rebuild to the design of Phillip Wyatt. It is this building that survives today.

The priory was sold out of the Braddyll family in 1854, and in 1878 it was acquired by a Scottish syndicate for conversion to a hydropathic health resort.

In 1929, it was purchased by the Durham Miners' Welfare Committee, who used it as a convalescent home until 1972. There then followed a 4 year period when it was practically unoccupied. Minimum maintenance left the building prey to the elements and dry rot ravaged much of the structural and decorative timber.

In 1976 it was occupied by the Manjushri Institute who intend to establish a college for Buddhist studies. The institute is working strenuously to restore the priory to its former glory.

Coniston, Brantwood

Charles Hudson was a mountaineer and founder member of the Alpine Club. The first successful climb of Mont Blanc was made by a team of young Englishmen of which Hudson was a member. This notable career came to an end when he was killed in the disastrous descent of the Matterhorn after the party, led by Wymper, had conquered the mighty mountain.

Hudson was one of the interesting owners and tenants who have occupied Brantwood. Another was William Linton, who made the house his home in May 1852. Linton, artist, poet and political writer, was first and foremost a wood engraver. He set up his own press and, with the help of friends, printed several republican journals. His domestic life was unfortunate; widowed twice and with a third marriage failed, he emigrated to America in 1866 to begin a new life.

John Ruskin, writer on art and architecture, bought Brantwood from Linton in 1871 and lived here until his death in 1900. Ruskin's early fame came when he championed J.M.W. Turner's work — an action that placed him at the helm of art criticism. He is remembered also for introducing the work of Tintoretto to the British public and for his efforts in establishing the pre-Raphaelites. The village museum contains some of Ruskin's drawings.

Ruskin's interests extended beyond art to the study of political and social economy. His book, *Unto This Last,* was acclaimed by Gandhi and George Bernard Shaw, and its influences are still felt today.

The 5¼ mile Coniston Water, is the scene of many water speed record breaking attempts including that of Donald Campbell in 1967, which resulted in this famous son of a famous father losing his life. A memorial now stands by the lake.

Cowan Bridge

Drivers speeding along the busy country highway between Ingleton and Kirby Lonsdale pass through Cowan Bridge with a blink of an eye.

Indeed visitors may for a moment wonder where the 'Bridge' is as recent road-widening hides it well. By its side stands a row of pretty cottages. On the gable of the cottage, there is a plaque which reads 'Maria, Elizabeth, Charlotte and Emily Brontë lived here as pupils of the Clergy Daughters' School 1824-25, *the school was moved to Casterton* 1833'. This quiet unassuming country cottage is known as 'Low Wood School of Jane Eyre'.

During the week, the young Brontë children studied here and no doubt played by the stream and round about the bridge, making friends with their neighbours' children from the picturesque cottages opposite.

Sundays were different; they would walk to the church at Tunstall for matins and evensong, eating what was left of their packed lunch in the porch chamber.

Croston

For many centuries the moods of the river Yarrow have dictated the lives of the people of Croston and, on numerous occasions, the river has taken their lives. The land is so low-lying that the frequent flooding has often made it impossible for the faithful to attend their church.

Croston has been an important Christian settlement since 651, when St Aiden's missionaries set up their ancient cross, broken many centuries ago and replaced in recent times. It stands at the end of a cobbled eighteenth century Church Street, where the houses back on to the river bank. At the end of Church Street is the venerable church with its tall tower slightly out of true. Between the church and the river stands a school on the site of one founded in 1283 and licenced by John of Gaunt. The school was given a free endowment by John Heit in 1660, only to be ejected two years later during the Commonwealth.

Croston, with Rufford, were once the chief suppliers of flax to the young textile industry in south east Lancashire. That was until the sixteenth century, when demand out-paced supply.

Croston was also famous for its market fairs with the indispensable ingredients of processions, bands playing, drinking, dancing, and general merrymaking.

Croxteth Hall

The Molyneux family home was at Sefton and in 1446 the Crown gave them Croxteth, where a house was built and the lands developed.

This was a family with strong military traditions and distinctions, but often dogged by minorities. Not until 1611 did they acquire their first hereditary title when Richard Molyneux was made a baronet. The second baronet, also a Richard, became a viscount in 1628. It was the eighth viscount who was made Earl of Sefton in 1771.

The Queen Anne wing of the house was added by the fourth viscount in 1702. Further building in 1874 and 1902 has left the Hall with two grand staircases.

It was the death of the seventh earl in 1973 that brought an end to the Molyneux family at Croxteth. The Hall and half the estate was given to the City of Liverpool and is now in the care of the Merseyside County Museums, and it is hoped that the Hall will be opened eventually to visitors.

The land is now a country park. Much of it is open to the public, while the remainder is being developed as a woodland nature reserve and the re-establishment of the old dairy farm.

Downham

To the north of Pendle Hill lies Downham, one of the prettiest villages in the county — indeed in the whole country!

The church and hall are side-by-side next to the little green which still has its stocks. Nearby are the inn and post office to complete this hilltop village.

Down the gradient, past an assortment of Tudor, Jacobean and Georgian houses, the road runs by the river, over the bridge, and on towards Pendle.

The Dinelays were the first manorial lords, succeeded in 1559 by the Asshetons, to whom must go the credit for making and preserving the village we see today.

Not only beautiful, Downham is a living working place based on agriculture, and is the home of a pedigree Ayrshire herd. Signs of weavers' cottages show evidence of an earlier industry. It is also progressive, being one of the first villages to have piped water and underground electricity cables.

Over the hill towards Clitheroe is the constant reminder of how fragile is the peace of this village, for Downham is built on one of the best deposits of limestone in the country!

29

Eccleston

The Old English word *écles* means a church, and place names such as Eccles, Eccleston and Great Eccleston suggest the establishment of Christian communities either before or during the early stages of Anglian settlement.

On the banks of the river Yarrow, Eccleston possesses an ancient church, beautifully set among tall trees and an immaculately kept grave yard. The sandstone tower (slightly out of true) with its four weather-cocks, looks warm and friendly. Close by is the sandstone bridge across the Yarrow and the water mill which, for generations, ground the locally produced corn.

The land around was once owned by Norman barons and, through the centuries, it has passed to many distinguished families such as the Garnetts, Dacres, Dicconsons, Molyneux and Wrightingtons.

The village grew and changed considerably during the last century after Messrs Smally opened their weaving mill, and the modern development has been even more dramatic. The village is very much a part of the twentieth century, yet it still retains enough character and community spirit to win the Best Kept Village Competition.

Edisford   Bridge

here was a ford across this wide shallow stretch of
e Ribble long before Clitheroe had its castle and charter.

Not all the travellers who crossed here were welcome. In
137, a horde of Scots, led by William Fitzduncan, were feared
nd disliked by both the local inhabitants and the Norman
arrison. For the first time, the population and occupation
rce were united in a common cause, and the Scots were
efeated at Edisford.

In the fourteenth century, a weir was built up stream from
Edisford to drive three water wheels. The increased water level
covered the much used 'Brungerley Hippings' and, therefore, a
bridge was built. The mill was demolished in 1967.

The luckless king, Henry VI, came this way in 1464. After
staying in hiding with the Pudseys at Bolton Hall, and
a brief stop at Waddington Hall, he was ambushed by the
Talbots of Bashall while attempting to cross the river by way of
the stepping stones.

31

Fairfield Moravian Settlement

The Moravian Church was founded in Bohemia by the followers of John Hus in 1457, and is the oldest Free Church in Europe. Moravian missionaries arrived in England in 1732 and played an important part in the Evangelical Revival during the eighteenth century.

The Fairfield community was established in 1785; one of a number of settlements which were established as places 'where Moravians might live and follow their private avocations'.

It was a self-governed community, planned and built b the people who lived there, basing their lives preaching and farming and the women gained fame f their fine embroidery. The village was laid out in simple formal plan, centred on the church, with th Sisters' and Bretherens' houses on either side. Th community also built individual houses around Fairfie Square; mainly Georgian they are, like the church, pla and elegant in style, and the village atmosphere is one unity, peace and gentility.

Fleetwood, Rossall School

This was originally the home of the devout Catholic Allan family. Cardinal Willaim Allan fled to Flanders on the accession of Elizabeth I and, in 1568, established a College at Douai. While he was training priests for mission work in England, Elizabeth was pursuing a vigorous persecution of the Lancashire Catholics.

After it became the home of the Fleetwoods, most of this ancient house was destroyed by the sea. The family moved to Hackensall Hall, having already acquired three quarters of the estates there. (See *Hackensall Hall).*

In 1733, heiress Margaret Fleetwood married into the Hesketh family but it was not until 1831 that the name Fleetwood-Hesketh appeared, after Peter Hesketh had obtained a royal licence. It was Peter Hesketh who founded the resort of Fleetwood, helping to bring in the railway. His grand vision for Fleetwood never came to pass — Liverpool put paid to it as a port; even so, its fishing fleet grew from strength to strength.

In 1843 the house at Rossall became a school for the sons of gentry and clergy.

Foxdenton Hall

There have been at least three manor houses known as Foxdenton Hall, the first owners of which were the de Traffords. In 1215, Richard de Trafford conferred the lordship and manor of Chadderton upon his second son, Godfrey and when Richard's grand-daughter, Margaret, married John de Radclyffe of Radclyffe Tower and Foxdenton, the Hall passed into that family as a dowry.

In 1620, William Radclyffe built the second Hall on the site, in the half-timbered style. Loyal supporters of Charles I, both William and his heir were killed at Edgehill in 1642. His second son, also called William, was knighted on the battlefield at Lostwithiel.

The Renaissance style building that survives today was built by Alexander Radclyffe and is a fine example of late seventeenth and early eighteenth century tastes. The Classical doorway, hipped stone roof, and prominent cornice, suggest it is a generation earlier than nearby Alkrington Hall.

There are surviving reminders of the old 1620 Hall. The present day basement and some panelling in the entrance hall are of the old building, but other panelling dates from 1700, and the chimney pieces with ornate plasterwork friezes are typical mid-eighteenth century examples.

Furness Abbey

In 1123, Stephen, count of Boulogne and Mortain, and later King of England, presented a site at Tulketh near Preston to the monks of the Order of Savigny, an order that in 1147 became part of the Cistercians. The monks stayed only four years at Tulketh before moving to the more remote Furness.

The abbey's possessions included most of the Furness peninsular, excluding Cartmel. Later, the holdings were increased by gifts and purchases of land stretching far into the Lake District and Yorkshire, but it was the development of Piel harbour and the establishment of daughter houses that significantly spread the abbey's influence into Cumberland, Yorkshire, Lincolnshire, Ireland and the Isle of Man.

For four centuries the monks ruled Furness like princes, dividing their lands into Granges from which they managed the outlying estates. With land both arable and rich in iron ore, together with later development of sheep rearing, the abbey became the second wealthiest Cistercian house in England.

In the Middle Ages, Furness, as a border district, suffered many raids from the Scots. The abbott paid Robert the Bruce a ransom for the safety of Furness and made him a guest of the abbey. But the monks also took active defence measures against the Scots, enlarging Piel Castle, building a tower overlooking their market town of Broughton, and establishing a beacon hill above the abbey.

Everything came to an end on 9 April 1537 when, under pressure, the brethren signed everything over to the King, Henry VIII.

Gawthorpe Hall

Off the main Padiham-Burnley road, down a long tree-lined drive, stands a fine Tudor mansion, the late home of the Shuttleworth family.

The original buiding on the site was a fourteenth century tower, with 8ft thick stone walls, and the construction of the mansion was started in 1599, under the watchful eye of Laurence Shuttleworth who, in his account books, kept details of the materials used, and even the tradesmen's names.

The Shuttleworths have a long history of government service both local and national. Not a martial family, they have however, been involved with war. Parliamentarian Richard Shuttleworth's efforts to avert civil war in 1642 were unsuccessful. Later, he and his son organised the Calder and Pendle cells of anti-Royalists, with Gawthorpe as the military headquarters.

The Hall has extended hospitality to kings and queens, politicians and literary figures. Richard Cobden and John Bright made speeches in the garden, and Charlotte Bronte did not resist the temptation to cross the border from Yorkshire to visit Gawthorpe.

Visitors still come to the Hall, which is now national property and a study centre. It houses the Rachel Kay Shuttleworth Collection of custome, lace, and woven and printed textiles.

Gisburn

This is a village that has grown alongside the main highway linking Lancashire and Yorkshire, where cattle dealers from both counties met to do business, or to watch the annual steeplechase.

The Romans passed near here on their way between York and Ribchester and centuries later, in 1464, Henry VI came to Bracewell for a secret meeting with the Tempests, the loyal Lancastrians.

Gisburn has an ancient church, inns, cottages and houses, stretching in origin from the sixteenth to nineteenth centuries. One of its inns, The White Bull, is named after the breed of huge white cattle that once roamed wild in Gisburn Park, for long the ancestral home of the Listers. One member of the family built his own inn, the Ribblesdale Arms, in 1635.

During the Civil War, Prince Rupert, following his successful Royalist campaign in Lancaster, marched his army up the Ribble Valley to the ignominy of Marston Moor in 1644.

After the start of the Second Civil War, Cromwell had to march down the Ribble Valley to Preston in August 1648, after wrongly anticipating that Hamilton and his Scottish army would march through Yorkshire in support of the king.

General Wills, leading the Hanovian troops, came down the valley during the Jacobite troubles of 1715.

There is now no better place than Gisburn to eat and drink, its many inns having refreshed countless travellers through the centuries.

37

Glasson Dock

Lancaster has been served with several ports through its long history.

Sunderland Point as an outer port was at the mercy of the weather and had the disavantage of being cut off by the sea twice daily.

St George's Quay on the bank of the Lune and in the shadow of the castle, always had navigational problems and the end came when the river started to silt up in the eighteenth century.

The building of Glasson Dock was financed by Lancaster merchants. A mooring used by the Lancaster Port Commissioners, it needed Acts of Parliament of 1738 and 1749 to cause the construction of a wall and quays. Between 1783 and 1791, a dock was built to accommodate 25 large merchant ships, but the main develoment came with the extension of the Lancaster Canal to Glasson in 1826 and, with it, a large canal basin with direct access to the main dock.

This made Glasson almost unique, it being one of the few locked docks in the country. Heavy wooden gates maintained a constant water level in the dock, and a further lock connected the canal basin. Larger ships could unload directly into barges moored alongside and smaller vessels could continue their voyages along the canal as far as Preston and Kendal.

The building of the railways to ports such as Preston, Fleetwood and Morecambe led to Glasson's rapid decline. Nevertheless, it is still a working port and, increasingly, a haunt of weekend sailors.

Goosenargh, Chingle Hall

his moated hall built in 1260 to the plan of a cross, near the
te of a Roman fort, is reputedly the most haunted house in
ngland; visitors frequently report the apparitions of two
onks.

In 1620, the priest John Wall was born here; martyred at
orcester in 1679 and canonised a few years ago.

In the days when death was the penalty for being caught

holding mass, secrecy was of the utmost. In order to inform
friends that the service was about to be held, a lighted candle
was placed at the small window in the porch.

The Hall was restored by the present owner, Mrs Howarth,
and her late husband. Peeling away the decor and trappings of
the centuries, they found ancient fireplaces, timbers from
Viking ships, four priest-holes, an old chapel, altars and a pre-
Reformation cross.

Hackensall Hall

The Romans came here for rock salt; so, too, did the present owners of the estate, Imperial Chemical Industries.

Hackensall takes its name from the settlement of the Viking Haakon who must have been well aware of its military importance in relation to the surrounding topographical features, as Major Ainsworth, the present occupier of the Hall, points out.

King John awarded the estate to Geoffrey the Crossbowman for services rendered, and the property passed through the male line of the family until the fifteenth century, when it was inherited by a daughter. On her death the estate was divided between her four daughters.

The Fleetwoods acquired three-quarters of the estate and moved here after the destruction of their home at Rossall. In 1656 they ordered the building of the Jacobean style Hall on the site of the earlier moated house.

The Hall is now privately owned and is enjoyed by the members of the Knott End Golf Club.

Haigh Hall

The land in the north of England was constantly the subject of dispute with the Scots; Lancashire was unable to resist the countless Scottish raids, part of the county's weakness stemming from the bitter rivalry between the land owning gentry.

In 1297, Thomas of Lancaster chose Robert Holland as his most trusted adviser. Robert was made a knight, then a baron, and his estates grew, much to the anger of his neighbours.

In 1315 Sir Adam Banastre of Sherington and Charnock Richard was joined by Sir William Bradshaigh, Sir Henry Lea and others, on an expedition of vengeance and gain. They rode to Wigan, failed to take Liverpool Castle, returned to Warrington and thence moved to Manchester.

Meantime, Robert Holland and the Sheriff, Sir Edmond Neville, raised a force of men, meeting and defeating Banastre and his friends at Deepdale near Preston.

Banastre, Lea and many others were executed on the field of battle but Sir William Bradshaigh escaped and went into exile.

Bradshaigh's wife, Lady Maud, was the great grand-daughter of Hugh le Norreys who, in 1188, owned both Speke and Haigh Halls. When she married Sir William, she took Haigh Hall with her as part of her dowry. Then, thinking her husband dead, she married again. Lady Mabel became famous because of her penance to 'Mab's Cross'.

41

Hall I' Th' Wood, Bolton

This is a fascinating house and museum in its own right. The Hall started its life in the late fifteenth century; a half-timbered house with a thatched roof, farm buildings and a water-powered mill, all surrounded by woods.

This was the home of the Brownlow family who added a stone-built wing in 1591, and Alexander Norris added the 'Norris Wing' during the seventeenth century. Lord Lever-hulme bought and restored the Hall before presenting it to the Bolton Corporation in 1920.

The Hall's fame stems from its associations with Samuel Compton who was born in 1753 at nearby Firwood Fold. It was while he was at the Hall that he developed his important invention, the 'mule', adopting the principles of Hargreaves' 'Spinning Jenny' and Arkwright's water frame, but adding five years of his own work and touch of genius. (See *Higher Mill Museum*).

Compton's 'mule' revolutionised the cotton industry and made countless fortunes. Yet Sam was to spend the later years of his life struggling to make ends meet, living on an annuity of £63 from a public subscription organised by his friends. In retrospect, it seems incredible that this homely genius never took out a patent on his invention.

Halton

An ancient village on the steep hills north of one of the loveliest stretches of the river Lune, and known as the Crook of Lune.

After the departure of the Romans, Lancaster decreased in importance and Halton became the administrative centre. North of the Ribble the land was divided into two *wapentakes,* Amounderness and Eurvicscire (Yorkshire). This land, owned by Earl Tostig, King Harold's brother, included areas we know as Furness, Cartmel, Kendal and Lonsdale. In 1065-66, Tostig's enemies ruthlessly invaded the area and Harold defeated his brother at Stamford Bridge a few days before the Battle of Hastings. Three years later, in 1069, William the Conqueror's men devastated the land when they 'harried the North' as punishment for revolt.

Tostig's Halle crowned the mound that overlooks Halton church.

Amounderness was allocated to Roger of Poitou, and William Rufus added Furness, Cartmel and Lonsdale. Roger considered Lancaster a better place than Halton from which to rule, and built his castle there, thus marking the birth of the county.

In Halton's churchyard can be found a Norse preaching cross, marking the place of worship until such time as a church could be built. Inscribed on one side is the Ascension of Christ, on the other is the story of Sigurd and Volsung, showing how Christianity and pagan beliefs existed side-by-side.

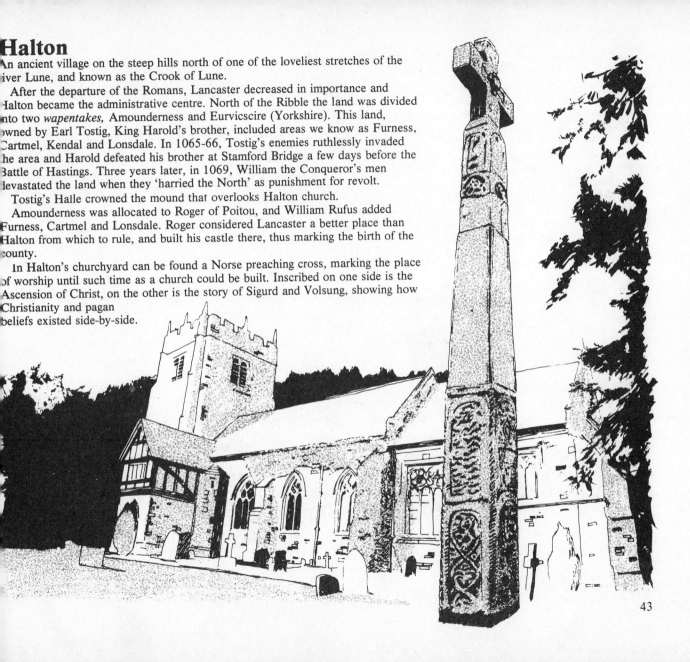

43

Hawkshead

Prehistoric man roamed the fells, but it was not until the tenth century that the Norsemen came and established the first recognisable settlement at Hawkshead; Norse farmers in search of new land.

For over 400 years the High Furness was administered by the monks of Furness Abbey, making Hawkshead their head quarters until the Dissolution.

Archbishop Edwin Sandys, born at Estwiate Hall, secured parish status for Hawkshead in 1578, and founded its grammar school in 1585 where William Wordsworth and his two brothers studied while lodging with Ann Tyson. Her cottage, with its outside staircase, is just off the Main Street, in the centre of the village.

In Elizabethan times, the church was so poor that it was unable to maintain and minister. Unorthodox religious leanings developed and, in the mid-seventeenth century, the new Quaker movement found a strong local following. The church is more fortunate today, and its good peal of bells can be heard a long way up the valley.

Having been isolated for so long, the village is unique. In the height of the holiday season the village overflows with tourists, which is a mixed blessing to the local community.

Hawkshead Courthouse

For about four centuries, vast lands in this district were owned and administered by the Cistercian monks from Furness Abbey. To facilitate the administration, Granges, like that of Hawkshead, were set up in the outlaying estates, where sheep and cattle rearing and woodland industries provided substantial revenue for the abbey in late medieval times.

The dissolution of Furness Abbey by Henry VIII caused disruption to the daily life of the people. After some years of uncertainty, a Code of Customs and Byelaws of 1586, in the reign of Elizabeth I, brought a foundation of regularity to the area's population, which was stregthened in 1606 with the granting of Letters Patent to Hawkshead to hold a market — an indispensable basis for any prosperity in those days.

Life in the valley was not easy; several outbreaks of plague and smallpox ravaged the population, and there were bitter feelings caused by split loyalties during the Civil War. Without roads for vehicular traffic, it was an isolated region until the opening of the turnpike. But it was the birth of the railway that brought real change. Trains carried visitors whose coming and going meant that Hawkshead's insular character had gone for ever.

Heaton Hall

The Holland family of Heaton and Denton owned this estate until 1683 when the heiress, Elizabeth Holland, married Sir John Egerton. It was their grandson, Sir Thomas Grey Egerton, who built a brick house at Heaton in about 1750.

His son, another Thomas, commissioned James Wyatt to design the house that survives today. The design, exhibited in 1772, was Wyatt's first country house and one of his three important houses in the Neo-Classical style, and was basically a remodelling of the older house, which can be seen to the north side.

Heaton Hall (originally called Heaton House) is considered to be the finest of its period in the north-west. The setting is six hundred acres of parkland with fine views towards Manchester and the Pennines. The park, with its lake and ponds, has more than the usual outlying buildings of stables, lodges and a temple, with recent additions of a GPO tower and the reconstructed facade of Manchester's old Town Hall.

Sir Thomas was made Baron Grey de Wilton in 1784, and Viscount and Earl of Wilton in 1801. The titles passed via his daughter Eleanor, to her second son. Thomas, a celebrated sportsman of his generation who held a series of race meetings in the park between 1827 and 1838, himself participating as an amateur jockey. The races were transferred to Aintree in 1839.

Hesketh Bank

The land to the north and south of the Ribble estuary is crossed by dikes, ditches and straight-as-ruler-edge roads; wide open green fields and vast full skies.

This was once untamed marshland; a no-mans land of will-o'-the-wisps. A place locals travelled by boat as much as by road; where villages were built on higher ground, mounds that frequently became islands (see *Bretherton*). In the eighteenth century, far seeing landowners such as the Ecclestons, Farmers, Heskeths, Fleetwoods, Cliftons and Hoghtons drained and reclaimed the land that was to become the market garden of Lancashire.

An early but unsuccessful attempt at land drainage was made by the Fleetwoods in 1692, but a century later the Ecclestons' schemes proved more fruitful due to the ingenuity of John Gilbert.

In the eighteenth and nineteenth centuries, Hesketh Bank even had its share of seaside visitors.

The greatest change to the landscape south of the Ribble came with the draining of Martin Mere. A price had to be paid and much has been lost; the sanctuary for wild life has been almost destroyed but for the protected nature reserves.

Hest Bank

Long before the turnpike roads, the railways and the motorways, the highway to the north led across the sands of Morecambe Bay. Robert the Bruce and Bonnie Prince Charlie came this way, as did the Romans centuries before.

The tall spire of Bolton-le-Sands was the guiding landmark when making the crossing between Hest Bank and Kents Bank — an adventure that had to be made at low tide with the help of guides from the priories of Carishead and Cartmel, until the duty was taken over by the duchy in the sixteenth century.

Travellers crossed in convoy; on foot, in waggons and on horseback, resembling some desert merchant's caravan. Not all made the crossing safely and those who perished in the fast incoming tides were buried in the grounds of Cartmel.

The hazardous crossing was part of the arterial route until the railways came this way in the 1840s. Today, Hest Bank has one of the busiest main lines in the land, but the sound of the trains does not deter the bird life of Morecambe Bay's nature reserve.

Heysham, St Patrick's and St Peter's

There is a legend of a ship-wrecked stranger staggering ashore and deciding to build his cell here. The year was AD 440 and the man was St Patrick.

Around this quiet and proud holy place, St Patrick's Chapel, are the graves of the great and saintly. Many are carved out of bedrock, but the tombstones are missing and the graves empty; small socket holes mark the locations for the stone crosses.

Probably it was seventh century Anglian settlers who gave Heysham its name and who, after adopting Christianity, built St Peter's below St Patrick's, in a spot out of sight from the raiding Vikings. Later, Viking settlers from Ireland established themselves along the Bay; being Christians, they joined with the local inhabitants in worship at the little church, which celebrated its 1,000th anniversary in 1967.

One of the church's greatest treasures is the tenth century hogback tomb cover of some otherwise forgotten Norse warrior.

The old village of Heysham has great charm. A walk down to the seashore on a quiet sunny summer's evening, with the little church bell calling the faithful to evensong, is one of the pleasantest journeys through time that I know.

Higher Mill Museum, Rossendale

To many people around the world Lancashire means cloth; King Cotton in particular. Yet wool was spun and woven long before cotton, and the textile trade was a lively and well organised cottage industry by Tudor times (see *Colne*).

Men were always looking for ways to increase production and profit; water power being used for 'fulling' as early as the twelfth century, but it was Arkwright's water frame that made large scale power spinning a possibility. Each new invention was just as unpopular as the last and, though expensive to install and unreliable, made the disliked factory system inevitable (see *Caldervale*).

The building of Higher Mill Museum was built by the Turners in 1789 and is one of the oldest wool textile finishing mills left in Lancashire. The museum contains early exam- ples of spinning wheels, hand cards, Hargreaves' spinning jenny, Arkwright's catching machines, drawframes, water-twist frames and much, much more. An 18ft diameter water wheel, installed in about 1850, drove pairs of fulling stocks (large wooden hammers) until 1954. Demonstrations of fulling and other processes can be seen by visitors to the museum, which is situated just off Holcombe Road, Helmshore, Rossendale. It is advisable to check the times of opening for visiting. (Telephone: Rossendale 26459).

Hoghton Tower

Built by Thomas de Hoghton between 1562 and 1565 on ground overlooking the river Darwen, on land still rich in sport and good hunting.

Sir Thomas was rich, landowning, warlike and faithful to the Church of Rome. He harboured Jesuits and was an associate of Cardinal Allen. Sir Thomas died in exile in 1580.

Between 1589 and 1630, Hoghton was owned by the protestant Sir Richard who, in 1617, entertained James I at one of the most lavish and costly of royal jamborees, involving himself in considerable personal debt.

The king sported with the Holcambe Hunt, evidently enjoying himself for he afterwards granted a Royal Warrant — the 'privilege of wearing the king's own scarlet livery and the right to hunt . . . *forever.*'

The incident involving James dubbing a joint of beef as 'Sir Loin' is said to have occurred while the monarch was banqueting in the Great Hall of Hoghton.

Sir Richard was succeeded by Sir Gilbert in 1630. At the outbreak of the Civil War he fought on the side of the King, but his son and heir was a Cromwellian. In 1643, the Royalist stronghold was taken by the Roundheads who destroyed the central Tower.

Sir Henry de Hoghton, who succeeded in 1710, fought the Jacobites at Preston in 1715, and in 1745 he opposed the Young Pretender.

Holker Hall

The magnificent ancestral home of the Prestons, the Lowthers, the Dukes of Devonshire and now the Cavendish family.

Mr and Mrs Cavendish and their family live here all year round, occupying the old west of the Hall. The new wing — to the public — was completely destroyed by fire in 1871, and it took the 7th Duke of Devonshire over three years to rebuild what the fire had destroyed in 3½ hours.

The Hall contains one of the finest collections of furniture and works of art to be seen anywhere. Queen Mary loved the house and stayed here in 1937.

All the owners of Holker have improved and shaped the land. They were agriculturists, reclaimers of mosses and road builders. The Cavendish family have also been great tree planters, as witnessed by the larches, giant monkey-puzzle trees and the cedars of Lebanon.

Holker is set in its own superb parkland, a working estate with a thriving herd of deer. All round is the rich green and gold of agriculture yet, not that many years ago, the nearby villages of Cark and Flookburgh were coastal, with shrimping and fishing as the industry and the safe transportation of 'oversands' travellers across the Leven Channel providing extra income.

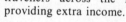

Hornby

Situated between two fordable rivers, the travellers' highway has always passed through the village of Hornby, a centre of valley life and defence stronghold since the days of the Vikings.

The castle was built in the twelfth century by the de Montbegon family. Since then it has passed through several ownerships: the de Burghs, the de Nevilles, and the Harringtons. Sir Thomas Harrington and his son died at the Battle of Wakefield in 1460, fighting on the side of the Yorkists. Later, the castle and estates were inherited, through marriage, by the Stanley family.

Many times has the valley been ravaged by raiding Scots, and it is scarcely surprising that a large force of local men followed Sir Edward Stanley's banner on a ride north; an expedition that culminated in the Battle of Flodden in 1513. For his part in the campaign, Sir Edward was installed with the Order of the Garter, and the title of Lord Monteagle. It was Monteagle's grandson who uncovered the Gunpowder Plot, and he had the honour of playing host to James I at the castle in 1617.

During the Civil War, as a Royalist stronghold, the castle was besieged by Colonel Assheton. On its capture, Cromwell decreed that it 'be so defaced or demolished that the enemy be prevented from making any further use thereof'.

Since then the castle has had many owners, all of whom have contributed to the undoing of Cromwell's words.

Hornby, St Margaret's Church

A church is known to have existed on this site since 1338, but it was Sir Edward Stanley, Lord Monteagle, hero of Flodden Field, who was responsible for the octagonal tower of 1513-14, in fulfilment, it is said, of a vow in honour of his patron saint, Margaret, after h[e] returned victorious from the Scottish wars.

Sir Edward did not live to see the completion of the work, and the chancel was unfinished when he died in 1524. He was buried in the Priory Church (site of Prior Farm), and the intention was to have his remains exhumed and transferred to St Margaret's whe[n] the chancel was built. It never was!

The church houses some interesting crosses. The 'Church Yard Cross', the height of which would have been about 12ft, is of pre-Norman origin. The 'Leaves and Fishes Cross', unique in England, although there are two similar examples in Ireland, is the upp[er] part of a cross that was originally about 5ft high. Thirdly, the pre-Norman 'Priory Cross' is a fragment of the lower arm of a small Greek cross.

Opposite the church in this tranquil village is the Presbytery of St Mary's Roman Catholic Chapel, once the home of Dr John Linyard, DD, one of the country's most illustrious historians, who wrote *History of England,* published in ten volumes between 1819 and 1830.

54

Hurstwood

On the moors above Burnley runs a 3,000 yr-old highway known as the long causeway. All round are the countless sites of camps, circles and burial mounds. Many of the villages and farmsteads have their origins in the Tudor period, when the inhabitants wrested a meagre living from these harsh moors by farming, spinning and weaving, sending the cloth to the market at Colne. Of these villages, Wycoller and Hurstwood have claims to fame for their literary connections.

To visit Hurstwood is to step back into the sixteenth century; nowhere can there be such well preserved Tudor dwellings still in domestic use. By the bridge is Hurstwood Hall, the proudest of the houses, built by Bernard Towley in 1579.

Down the lane to the right is Spenser's House, the cottage where the sixteenth century giant, Edmund Spenser, is thought to have stayed with his uncle during college vacations.

In 1576, Spenser retired to Hurstwood where he wrote verse in the pastoral vein in honour of his Rosalind, who has not been satisfactorily identified but was possibly Rose Dineley of Clitheroe.

Beyond the cottage is Tattersall's Tenement, a farm where Richard Tattersall made his first horse sale, before going on to establish the world-famous stables at Hyde Park Corner, London, in 1766. Tattersall, in association with the Prince of Wales, became owner of the *Morning Post* in 1788.

Kersal Cell

At number 1 The Shambles, now the Old Wellington Inn, on 29 February 1692, was born John Byrom, son of a well-to-do Manchester family. Five months after John's birth, Kersal Cell was bought by his father, Edward Byrom, a milliner. It was his cousin who built Byrom House in Quay Street and his son, Edward, one of the first of the city's bankers, who founded St John's Church.

Educated at Chester, the Merchant Taylors' School in London, and Trinity College, Cambridge and there taking a BA degree in 1711. John Byrom chose not to follow any of the family professions. Instead, he turned to the pen and invented his own system of shorthand: as an undergraduate he contributed to *The Spectator,* and published a poem that earned him instant fame. He earned his living by teaching shorthand and, in 1723, was elected a Fellow of the Royal Society.

In 1721, he married, setting up house in Hanging Ditch, Manchester. When his brother died he inherited the Kersal Estates.

A kind, clever, genial man of wit and good-humoured satire, Byrom started his journal in 1707 and continued it for the next 56 years. In politics he leaned towards the Jacobites, but steered a middle course in public life. Two of his achievements were that for a time he was 'poet laureate' of the John Shaw Club, and he wrote the words of the Christmas Hymn, *Christians Awake,* the original manuscript of which is in Chethams Library.

Knowsley Hall

The Hall passed to the ownership of the Stanley family through Isabel, the wife of Sir John Stanley. She inherited the estates of Lathom and Knowsley in 1390 from Sir Thomas Lathom.

In 1405, Sir John Stanley became Lord of Man, and his grandson, Sir Thomas, was made a baron in 1456. Sir Thomas, the second baron, married Lady Margaret Beaufort, the widowed mother of Henry Tudor. It was Sir Thomas' last minute yet decisive support of Henry Tudor at Bosworth, that secured the crown of England for Henry and the Earldom of Derby for Sir Thomas (see *Lathom Park Chapel*). Further estates were added after the battle of Stoke in 1487, when Lambert Simnel's bid for the throne was stemmed (see *Piel Castle*).

In 1495, Henry VIII visited his step-father's houses at Knowsley and Lathom. Derby built a new extension at Knowsley and paid for the rebuilding of Warrington bridge, so that the king and his party could cross the river.

Knowsley now has a well-known Safari Park set in the grounds. The hall is at present a police headquarters and is strictly private.

Lancaster Castle

This hill above the river Lune was of such strategic value that it was a defensive position even before the Romans decided to build their fort there. By the time the Normans arrived its importance had diminished to the extent that in Domesday it is recorded simply as part of Halton. William the Conquerer gave the lands — once held by Tostig, King Harold's brother — to a kinsman, Roger of Poitou, who built the great castle that survives today.

In 1189, Richard the Lionheart granted the castle and Honour of Lancashire to his brother John (later King John), one of the few kings to visit the castle and take a special interest in its affairs.

Granted to Henry Plantaganet in 1327, and thence to his son — again a Henry, who became the first Duke of Lancashire, with palatine jurisdiction, in 1351. Through his daughter Blanche, who was married to John Plantaganet (John of Gaunt), the castle passed in 1399 to their son, Henry of Bolingbroke.

Banished after quarrelling with his uncle, Richard II, Henry returned to raise an army and defeat Richard. He was elected King (Henry IV) and one of his edicts ensured that the Duchy became the private property of the monarch, and separate from the Crown.

Lancaster Castle, Shire Hall

Lancaster Castle has been a county prison from its earliest days. Criminals of all kinds have suffered and many have died here; Roman Catholics, Protestants, Quakers, those accused of witchcraft, debtors, and even lunatics, before asylums were instituted.

The ground floor of the keep accommodates the prison chapel, and the first floor the Old Shire Hall. The upper floor contains the Quaker Room so called because of the many of that faith who were imprisoned here.

Thomas Harrison carried out alterations and improvements in the late eighteenth century, including the present day Shire Hall and the Crown Court. The former is a semi-circular court room, on the walls of which is displayed a unique collection of coats-of-arms of Sovereign Constables of Lancaster Castle and the High Sheriffs, dating from the twelfth century. The Hall is regularly used as a Magistrates' Court and as a second Crown Court.

Until 1835, the Crown Court was the only Assize Court in Lancashire. It is said that more people have been sentenced to death here than in any other court in the kingdom.

Before rebuilding, executions took place on Lancaster Moor. Later the gallows were erected at Hanging Corner, facing the churchyard. Hanging Day was almost a holiday with up to 6,000 people assembled to watch the grisly scene.

Lancaster, Friends Meeting House

Almost in the shadow of the formidable Castle of Lancaster stands the quiet and unassuming Friends Meeting House, built in 1708.

The roots of the Quaker movement are in Lancashire. Although its founder, George Fox, was not a Lancashire man, it was on the summit of Pendle Hill that he had his vision in the Spring of 1652, and it was in Lancaster that he and his friends and followers were imprisoned. So many Friends were confined here that a room in the keep is known as the Quakers' Room.

Until his death their ally, Judge Thomas Fell, was able to protect them from the full force of persecution that was to follow.

It must be said that the Friends fared better than many others who were imprisoned in Lancaster 'for conscience sake'. Both Catholics and Protestants suffered here during the reigns of Henry VIII, Elizabeth I and Charles I. Many were hanged, disembowelled while still alive, decapitated and quartered; then, as a deterrent, their parts were displayed at the castle and other public places.

Lancaster Priory Church St Mary

From early times, church and castle have shared the same hill above the river Lune.

Beneath the church's foundations are the remains of a Roman basilica which had been left to the ravages of the invading tribes at the end of the occupation. In about the year 650, missionaries brought Christianity back to Lancaster and the ruins of the basilica became part of an important Saxon church which was later granted to the Benedictine Abbey of St Martin of Seez by Roger of Poitou, and a priory was founded.

Practically nothing remained of the early building after the construction of a new church in the fourteenth and fifteenth centuries.

Shortly after Henry V's suppression of foreign priories, Lancaster passed to the Brigittine Convent of Syon — a double covent for nuns and monks. Finally, in the wake of the Reformation, the priory church became the parish church of Lancaster.

A new tower was built in 1759 as a separate structure; only later was it connected to the main fabric.

Inside, the fourteenth century canopied choir stalls are among the most remarkable to be seen anywhere.

Lancaster, St George's Quay

From about 1680, Lancaster gained momentum as a thriving trading port, handling cargoes of tobacco, timber, sugar, rum and molasses from such widespread parts of the world as the West Indies, the Americas and the Baltic.

Shipbuilding followed with its attendant trades, making anchors, blocks, rope and sail. Naturally, industry developed in the town to utilise the imports: soap works, textile mills, sugar refineries and furniture workshops. Table baize, oilcloth, leather cloth and American cloth were also made in Lancaster;

two of the great names connected with these products, Jam Williamson and James Storey, leaving their marks by the bequests: Williamson Park, Lineside Park, the Town Hall now a museum, and the Storey Institute.

In the latter half of the eighteenth century, Lancaster as port was second only to Liverpool in both coastal and overse trade. The tall warehouses and the Customs House with Palladian facade of 1765, by Richard Gillow, are relics of th period of Lancaster's past.

By the quayside stands the Carpenter's Arms — named after
s regular clientel of ship's carpenters. It was here on market
nd fair days that unsuspecting lads were offered free drink
ntil, confused and incapable, king's shillings were dropped in
eir pockets and they were whisked away to waiting ships as
ictims of the press gang.

Relics of engineering history are nearby up river. The New
ridge, completed in 1788, was designed by Thomas Harrison
) carry mail coaches into the town. A few years later, in 1797,

John Rennie built the 600ft long aquaduct with its fine semi-
circular arches, to carry the Lancaster Canal.

The inherent navigational problems of the Lune caused the
building down river of the New Quay in the eighteenth century,
to accommodate the larger ships, but this was not enough to
win trade from the new ports with their deeper anchorages and
railway connections. Despite several schemes to improve
navigation and provide a railway, Lancaster had finally to
concede its role of major seaport.

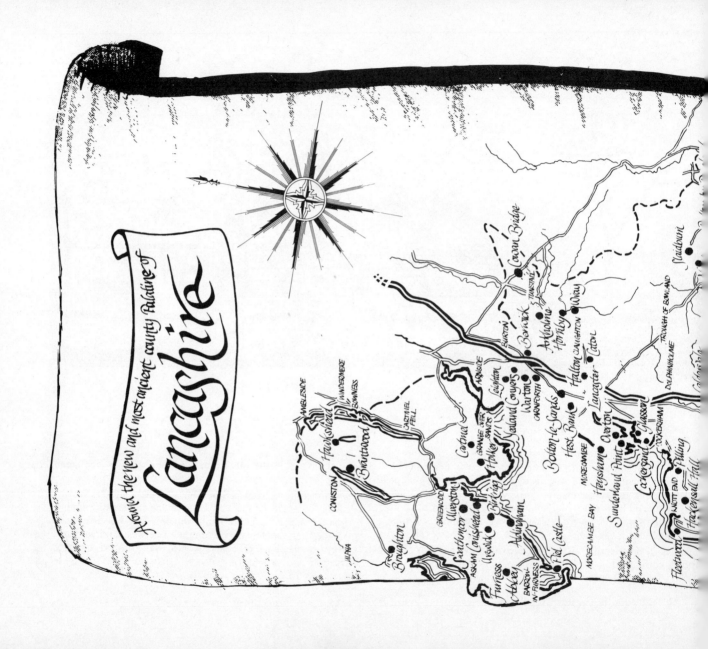
Around the new and most ancient county Palatine of *Lancashire*

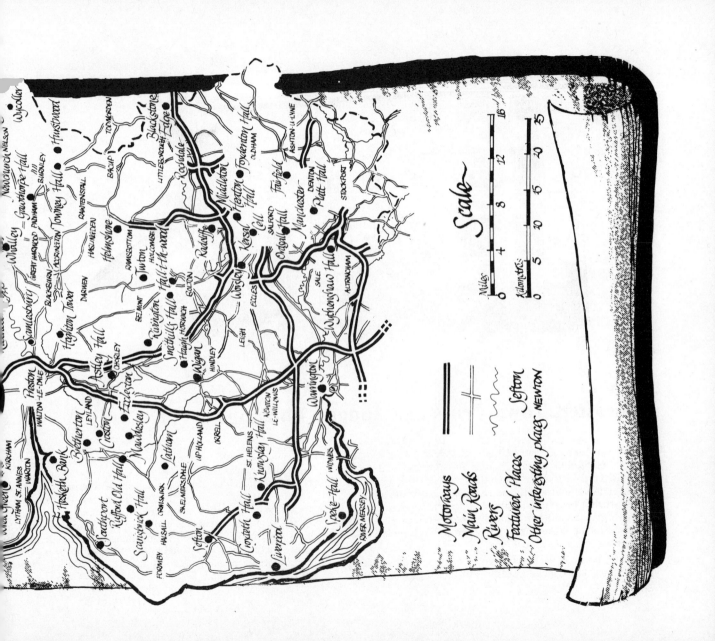

Scale

Miles
0   4   8   12   16

Kilometres
0   5   10   15   20   25

Motorways
Main Roads
Rivers
Featured Places   Sefton
Other interesting places   NEWTON

Wycoller
Newchurch NELSON
Husteroood
Gawthorpe Hall
Towneley Hall
Great Harwood PADIHAM
BURNLEY
BLACKBURN
Whalley
Salmesbury
Blackstone Edge
BACUP
TODMORDEN
Rochdale
Rawtenstall
HASLINGDEN
Helmshore
LITTLEBOROUGH
DARWEN
Middleton
Foxdenton Hall
OLDHAM
RAMSBOTTOM
Hoghton Tower
Kersal Heaton Hall
ASHTON-U-LYNE
BELMONT
HOLCOMBE
Cell Hall
FAIRFIELD
Turton
DENTON
SALFORD
Platt Hall
Rivington Hall
Hall-i-th-wood
Ordsal Hall
Manchester
STOCKPORT
Smithills Hall
BOLTON
Haigh HORWICH
WIGAN
WOLSLEY
SALE
Radcliffe
Astley Hall
CHORLEY
HINDLEY
EGCLES
Wythenshaw Hall
ALTRINCHAM
LEIGH
Euxton
PRESTON
WALTON-LE-DALE
Bretherton
LEYLAND
Croston
Mawdesley
ATHERTON
LE-WILLOWS
Warrington
LYTHAM St ANNES
KIRKHAM
WARTON
Hesketh Bank
Rufford Old Hall
UP HOLLAND
ORRELL
St HELENS
Southport
Scarisbrick Hall
Tatham
SKELMERSDALE
WIDNES
WAL GREEN
FORMBY
HALSALL ORMSKIRK
Sefton
Croxteth Hall
Knowsley Hall
Liverpool
Speke Hall
RIVER MERSEY

Lancaster, Town Cross and Judges' Lodgings

History surrounds us as we walk down Castle Hill. Castle Green with its eighteenth century houses of attorneys and court officials. To the left at the Town Cross stands the magnificent Georgian house that was the home of the Beaumonts until the 1820s, when it became the Judges' Lodgings. There is another fine georgian building in Church Street; a house that once belonged to the Duke of Hamilton and where Bonnie Prince Charlie was entertained in 1745.

One of the duties of the local gentry was to provide an escort for the Sheriff of Lancashire and visiting judges, assuring their safety when riding to Assizes. They supplied the Sheriff with food and wine for entertaining judges, and certain estates had to contribute hospitality and lodging for the Sheriff while he was on the King's Business. The Sheriff's duties were manifold, including the execution of writs, death sentences, preparing jury panels, and the safe custody and delivery of prisoners. A year as Sheriff was a considerable personal financial strain, despite the help to which he was entitled under the customs of the office, and eventually a small donation was available from the Duchy Purse.

Lathom Park Chapel

The Stanley family owned the Halls at both Knowsley and Lathom.

In 1485 Richard III faced Henry Tudor at Bosworth Field. The balance of the day was in the hands of Sir Thomas Stanley who had to make a fateful decision: who to support. Richard held his son as hostage, while Henry was his stepson and he had sympathy with the Tudor cause. Sir Thomas chose Henry; the battle was won and Richard killed. After the coronation Henry rewarded Sir Thomas with the Earldom of Derby.

Lathom Park Chapel was consecrated in 1500, built by Thomas Lord Stanley, Second Earl of Derby as a thanks offering for the benefits received after the battle.

During the Civil War sympathies in Lancashire were dictated by religious belief which had the effect of dividing the county. Tide of battle flowed first one way then the other, but by the end of 1643 the Royalists held only Lathom House and Greenhalgh Castle. Lathom was put to siege by Colonel Alexander Rigby in February 1944 and the Countess of Derby defended the house with only 300 men. Prince Rupert gave the Parliamentarians a harrowing time when he swept through Cheshire, attacked Stockport and Bolton, re-occupied Wigan, plundered Liverpool and freed Lathom; only to suffer later defeat at Marston Moor.

The Parliament forces soon recovered their losses and Lathom was again under siege, but the defenders managed to hold the house until December 1645, by which time the First Civil War was almost over.

The Second Civil War began in 1648 and the Scottish army, in support of Charles I, marched south and met Cromwell and his troops at Preston which resulted in a running battle as far as Warrington (see *Preston, Walton Bridge*).

A second Scottish army, this time supporting Charles II, invaded in 1651. The Earl of Derby, who was holding the Isle of Man, crossed to the mainland with some of his men to help. He raised an army of some 1,500 men but was defeated in August at Wigan Lane. Derby was taken prisoner after the Battle of Worcester and was tried at Chester; on the 16th October he was executed at Bolton. A month later his wife surrendered the Isle of Man, where she was imprisoned until the Restoration.

During the two sieges the chapel was both used and abused by the Roundhead troops, and suffered as a result. However, excellent restoration work makes the chapel and almshouses one of the most delightful spots in the county (see *Knowsley*).

Lathom House has been rebuilt twice but little remains of it today.

Leighton Hall

Although there have been twentyfour owners of this property which must have the most beautiful setting of all the houses in Lancashire, Leighton is best known as the home of the Gillow family.

In 1246 it was owned by Adam d'Avranches, from whom it passed to the Redurans, the Yealands, the Conyers, the Crofts, the Middletons, the Oldfields, the Hodgsons, the Townleys, the Worswicks, and thence to the Gillows, whose descendants, Mr and Mrs Reynolds, are the present owners.

All but one owner of Leighton has been a Roman Catholic, and a priest was always hidden here in penal times.

Sir George Middleton, distinguished cavalier and colonel of the Royalist army, was knighted and made a baronet on the same day in Durham in 1642. He was heavily fined in Cromwellian times for his loyalty to the Crown.

Another devotee to a cause was Albert Hodgson who, in the Jacobite uprising of 1715, was taken prisoner at Preston and his house at Leighton was sacked by Government troops.

Only traces of the Tudor and Jocobite residences remain; in 1763 an Adam style house was built on the site. It was replaced in 1800 in the Gothic style, the architect probably being the remarkable Harrison of Chester.

Liverpool

The first charter for the town was granted by King John in 1207, when a Norman castle stood on the site now marked by Queen Victoria's statue. A reconstruction of the castle ruins can be seen in Lever Park near Rivington.

Once Henry VII and Henry VIII had restored order in Ireland and at sea, the shipping trade increased. The growing textile industry needed Irish flax for mixing with wool, and there was a healthy export trade of finished textiles back to Ireland. Liverpool shipowners were able to handle this trade cheaper than those in Chester because, although Chester was the administrative centre of the northwest coast, in the fifteenth century it had suffered the setback of moving sands in the Dee Estuary which had partly blocked the river.

The Irish Rebellion in 1641, the English Civil War and Cromwell's campaign in Ireland, caused the Liverpool merchants to look further afield for trade and, during 1666-7, *The Antelope* sailed the first known voyage to Barbados, thus starting a new era in Liverpool's prosperity.

Small ships could anchor in a small estuary called The Pool, while larger vessels had to discharge their cargoes in Hoyle Lake. In 1703, several anchored ships were lost in a gale, prompting the council to build Thomas Steers' Dock at the mouth of The Pool; the dock being opened in 1715. Canning Place now marks the site of this original dock.

Liverpool is not Liverpool without the Mersey Ferry. In 1318, the Prior of Birkenhead had to provide lodgings and provisions for the people stranded on that side of the river, when the weather made the return journey impossible.

From the end of the seventeenth century, Liverpool shipowners were increasingly active in slave-trading, taking cloth, spirits, utensils and ornaments to Africa with which to barter for a human cargo. Once fully loaded, they raced for the West Indies, where the slaves were sold, and the ships returned home with sugar, tobacco and molasses, the captain and his owners making a handsome profit on each leg of the voyage.

Many merchants feared the end of the slave-trade but when it was finally abolished in 1807, Liverpool's trade actually increased, with the opening of new markets in South America, Africa and the Far East.

Liverpool has always had strong links with Manchester, and never stronger than when they shared the world's first public railway which opened in 1830 (see *Manchester, Liverpool Road Station*).

Lower Hodder Bridges

The Sherburnes paid Rodger Crossley, in Tudor times, the princely sum of £70 for building the old Cromwell Bridge.

It was in August 1648 that Oliver Cromwell and his model army of Ironsides are reputed to have passed this way en route for Preston to do battle with the Royalists. Although named after him, it is possible that he did not use the bridge at all. The River Ribble was not spanned between Edisford near Clitheroe and Walton Bridge outside Preston until the seventeenth century, and the crossing at Mitton was by ferry. It seems likely therefore that the Ironsides crossed the Ribble at Edisford Bridge and the Hodder at High Hodder. The latter bridge was replaced over a century ago.

Cromwell did however, lodge nearby at Stonyhurst Hall, owned by the Sherburnes. The family were known Royalists and, it is said Cromwell, unwelcome guest that he was, spent the night on a hard table, his men on guard and with pistols at the ready!

Mains Hall

Close to the River Wye, this ancient Hall was better known as Monks Hall, when it was a moated house belonging to the Hesketh family. The old barn still bears the initials of William and Margaret Hesketh, and the date 1686 is displayed in bricks projecting along its sides.

The Heskeths were Papists and related to Cardinal Allan of Rossall (see *Fleetwood*). They built secret hides and harboured priests in a wing of the house which vanished long ago. During the 1745 campaign, Scottish fugitives hid here with the pro-Stuart Heskeths.

In the eighteenth century the Hall went through radical alterations, including the removal of the top storey.

Maria Smith was married twice by the age of 25. Her second husband was Colonel Fitzhurbert who, through marriage, had links with the families of Brockholes and Heskeths. Mrs Fitzhurbert became the morganatic wife of George IV; but gossip forced her into hiding at Mains, while debts and the need to produce an heir caused the king to marry his cousin, Caroline of Brunswick, in 1795.

Manchester Cathedral

Although Manchester did not have a cathedral until 1847, it had long been an ecclesiastical centre, the Christian faith being brought to the area by Paulinus and Edwin of Northumbria.

A Saxon church was built on a bluff bounded on the west side by the 40ft wide 'Hanging Ditch'. Since no trace of Norman building is to be found on the site, it must be assumed that this church served for some many years.

In 1421, Thomas La Warre, Lord of the Manor, founded a College of Clergy, and the following year saw the start of the building of a new parish church of St Mary's, in the Perpendicular Gothic style.

The eighteenth and nineteenth century industrial growth brought enormous changes to Manchester, as it did to many other northern towns and cities. In the hundred years between 1752 and 1851, the population swelled from 18 to 445,000, made up mainly by immigrant workers. Mushroom building filled the gaps and spread from the medieval nucleus and the cathedral church was reduced in scale by the surrounding buildings.

The Victorians found it necessary to replace the original outside fabric of red Collyhurst sandstone with Derbyshire stone. In general the architecture was copied but certain additions were made: the height of the tower was increased, and the porches at the north and south sides were added. The ornate 'Victoria' porch and vestries were added in 1898. Chisel marks on the masonry supporting the tower arch must not be blamed on the Victorians; they reflect the carelessness of some earlier 'restoration'.

The area was badly mutilated in the 1940 air raids, with one bomb falling within a few feet of the cathedral's north east corner. Since the end of the war in 1945, a new Lady Chapel has been built and the Regimental Chapel restored. In the course of restoration, thousands of pieces of wood had to be let into the choir stall canopies but this does not impair their value as fine examples of the art of woodcarving.

Manchester, Castleford

In an area covered with so many marks of the Industrial Revolution, it is difficult to imagine that the Roman fort of Manucium once stood where the timber yard is now situated. Built on a sandstone bluff, sometime after AD 71, it occupied an area of about 5 acres. The fort was strongly defended in its later history and, like other Roman fortifications, a thriving civilian community grew up around it — the basis for what is now Manchester.

The Bridgewater Canal was opened in 1761, but the Castleford Terminus was not built until after the Hulme Hall estate had been purchased in 1764. In spite of industrial development, several buildings in the district survive from around this time.

Georgian and Victorian engineers carved their way through a piece of heritage, for when they linked the Bridgewater and Dale Street Canal basins in 1805, the short, well locked, stretch cut straight through the old Roman fort, as did the railways with their remarkable iron bridges a few decades later.

The canal is still extensively used as part of the popular Cheshire Loop. It is unique in that it is still privately owned.

Manchester, Cheetham's

Sharing the same sandstone bluff as the cathedral, these two buildings formed the nucleus from which the town of Manchester spiralled out.

It was originally the manorial Hall of the de la Warre family. Thomas de la Warre was a priest at the church and decided to establish a collegiate body for the training of priests. The conversion of the Hall was undertaken between 1422 and Thomas's death in 1426.

The college was dissolved in 1547 and the lands granted to the Stanleys, Earls of Derby. After the execution at Bolton of the Royalist Seventh Earl, the estate was forfeited to the state in 1651.

Humphrey Cheetham's executors purchased the Hall in 1654

to form a Bluecoat School and to establish a library. Through the years his library has gathered a massive collection of books on theology, natural science and architechture, eventually specialising in topography and history, particularly local history. At one time the rarest books were chained to the reading desks.

Some of its most distinguished visitors have included Engels, Marx and John Byrom. Indeed, the library inherited most of Byrom's books, among them his original manuscript for *Christians Awake.*

Today the old Hall hums to the music and laughter of young people, for it is now the home of the famous school of music.

Manchester, Free Trade Hall

In the nineteenth century life was hard for the unemployed, and little better for those who were in work. In Manchester cotton mills, men, women, and children toiled for fourteen hours a day without a break and for a pittance of a wage.

In August 1819, a large crowd gathered in St Peter's Field to hear speeches demanding changes in government attitude. Uneasy about the outcome of the demonstration, the authorities ordered the Manchester Yeomanry to break it up. The mounted troops needlessly slashed out at the crowd with their sabres and in the melee 6 people were killed and about 400 injured. This tragic event became known as 'Peterloo' — a sarcastic reference to the Battle of Waterloo.

The Free Trade Hall commemorates the city's most important contribution to national politics — the Anti-Corn League, founded by local men such as Richard Cobden and John Bright who advocated Free Trade and non-intervention between employer and employee. The repeal of the Corn Laws came in 1846, thanks to another Lancashire man, Sir Robert Peel.

The present building is the third Free Trade Hall, designed by Edward Walters and completed in 1856. Since 1858 it has been the home of Manchester's own Halle Orchestra. The interior was completely rebuilt after the heavy damage by wartime bombs.

Manchester, Liverpool Road Station

The county is so rich in early industrial relics and most Lancastrians probably see them all too frequently. They are probably even gladdened when they disappear, not realising their archaeological importance.

One of the most important and, at present, the most derelict, is the original Manchester terminus of the Liverpo[ol] and Manchester Railway, in Liverpool Road.

Plans for a railway connection between the two cities we[re] discussed in the early 1820s and, in spite of bitter oppositi[on] from the canal companies, landowners and even the Liverpo[ol] Corporation, Parliament finally passed an amended bill [in] 1826. Through the engineering genius of George Stephens[on] and the energetic enthusiasm of Henry Booth, the world's fir[st] public railway was ready for opening by the Duke [of] Wellington in September 1830.

The old station is a two-storey block with the platform on th[e] first floor. In 1844, the line was extended to Hunts Ban[k] (Victoria), carving its way through Salford on a massiv[e] viaduct. No longer a terminus, Liverpool Road became a good[s] station and all round this venerable railway relic can b[e] found some of the oldest warehouses in the city.

The original 1839 Manchester and Leeds Railwa[y] terminus at Oldham Road was demolished i[n] 1968. It, too, had been converted to [a] goods station when the line wa[s] extended to Victoria and som[e] of the old buildings remai[n] to be used fo[r] warehousing.

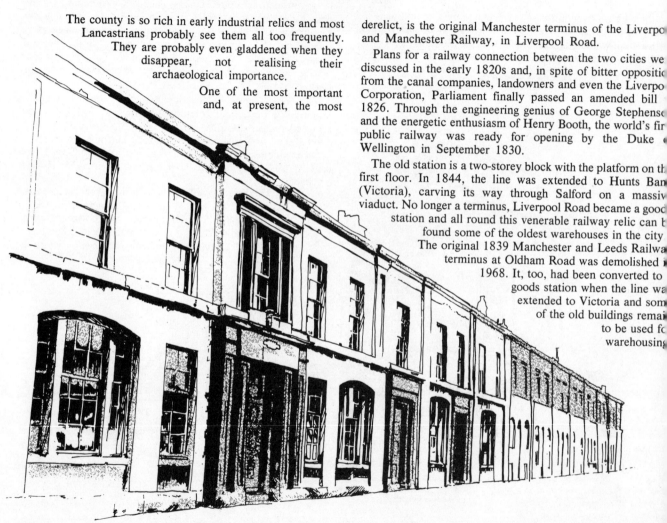

Manchester, Old Wellington Inn

Situated in the centre of the old Market Place, the inn is one of the few surviving timber-framed buildings in Manchester. The wartime *blitz* made sure of that, striking deep into the medieval centre of the city.

Reputedly built in 1328, it has, as a dwelling, been subtanitially altered down the centuries and was converted to an inn in 1830.

In the medieval market, where people met to gossip and sell their wares, a cross, pillory and stocks stood until 1815. Here also was The Boothes, a two-storeyed half-timbered structure with a courthouse and town hall on the upper floor — the town's first public building.

Not until the eighteenth century did Market Street, with its half-timbered buildings, reach as far as what is now Piccadilly. Beside the street ran an obnoxious stream which regularly overflowed, and by the old Market Place the street was only 5yds wide including the pavements. No wonder the wheels of carts frequently crushed people against the walls.

The Old Wellington Inn and the adjoining buildings have been raised 5ft to make them the centre piece of the Market Place Shopping Development.

Manchester, The Portico Library

Designed by Thomas Harrison and completed in 1806, the Portico Library, principal circulating library in Manchester until 1850, was situated in 'the most elegant and retired street in town'.

When the library was opened, England was at war, Trafalgar had been won, and both Pitt and Fox had died. Two of the subscribers were on the staff of the Manchester Infirmery, situated where Piccadilly Gardens are now. One, a physician, Dr John Ferriar, who drew attention to the wretched dwellings of workers in Manchester. The other doctor was Peter Mark Roget, whose *Thesaurus*, or at least part of it, was probably compiled in the library. Others included Robert Peel, destined to become Prime Minister and Richard Cobden of Anti-Corn League repute.

In 1819, not only was the news read in the library; from the front steps it could be seen in the making, as crowds marched past to St Peter's Field and the 'Peterloo Massacre'.

Manchester, St Ann's Church

The foundation stone of Manchester's second church was laid at Acresfield in 1709. There were 19 other eighteenth century churches but they did not survive the loss of their congregations.

Acresfield was once a cornfield where an annual fair was held from 1227 until 1823, when the residents complained that their shops were being over-run by pigs and cattle. In consequence, the fair was moved to Knott Mill.

A few yards away stands Cross Street Chapel, the oldest non-conformist place of worship in the city. Built in 1694, the original building was gutted in 1715 by a Jacobite mob. Rebuilt through a grant from Parliament, it was again destroyed in a Second World War air raid. The present building dates from 1959.

A preacher here in the nineteenth century was the Rev William Gaskell, the first honorary secretary of the Portico Library. His wife was the novelist, Elizabeth Gaskell, whose novel *Mary Barton* (1848), a story of factory life, made her famous.

Dominating St Ann's Square is the Royal Exchange, proudly boasting the international importance that Lancashire cotton once had. It is the third of Manchester's Royal Exchanges and the second on the present site. At its peak there were 11,000 members, representing every aspect of the textile industry, and was the world's largest place of assembly for direct business transactions.

An exciting free standing theatre has been built in the Great Hall, known as Theatre 69 and seating up to 700 people.

Manchester, St John's Street

A street originally occupied by leading merchants, that more or less marked the town's extent during the mid-eighteenth century. Nowadays, the fine Georgian front doors gleam in the summer sun with rows of proudly polished name plates, confirming the worthiness of the surgeons, physicians, consultants and eye specialists within, for this has become Manchester's equivalent of Harley Street.

It is said that one day in 1846, a certain father and daughter came to one of the houses. Waiting while her father had an eye operation, the girl wrote down, 'There was no possibility of taking a walk that day...', the first line of Jane Eyre.

The gardens opposite the Byrom Street end mark the site of St John's Church, built in 1768, which must have given the street a fine back drop. Alas, it was demolished in 1932, so the vista must be left to the imagination.

Turn right and walk to Quay Street. Along here is where Bonny Prince Charlie kept his artillery while stopping over in Manchester. The site is marked by a blue plaque.

At Quay Street, turn left and cross Byrom Street, where another blue plaque on the building ahead informs us that this was once the home of Richard Cobden (1804-65) statesman and originator of free trade.

Mawdesley

It is hard to decide where this large rambling village starts or ends; a village whose industry comprises farming, mining, quarrying and basket weaving. Each year, thousands of baskets were sent from Mawdesley to all parts of the country, the products of such weaving concerns as the Benthams, Mawdesleys and Cobhams, who grew their buff, green and white willow in the local moss. Now the Cobhams survive as the main producers of baskets, with imposing showrooms in the centre of the village.

With an expanding population, unlike many country villages, Mawdesley has a lively and thriving air, reflected by its new buildings, contrasting with one of its oldest, the Black Bull Inn, better known to locals by its other name, 'Hell Hob': a name probably derived from a giant poker weighing 16lbs, 'to poke the fire of a *hell hob*', the subject of many a drunken wager.

Middleton

The parish church of St Leonard's dates from the twelfth century, and it was the local born Thomas Langley, once Bishop of Durham, Cardinal and Lord Chancellor of England, who rebuilt and consecrated the church in 1412. Langley also founded the grammar school, the forerunner of Queen Elizabeth's School.

Between 1515 and 1524, the church was largely rebuilt, as a thanks offering by Sir Richard Assheton and his archers after winning distinction and victory at Flodden. The stained glass Flodden Window depicts Sir Richard, his wife, and sixteen archers. A later rebuilding took place in the seventeenth century when the unique wooden steeple was constructed.

Some excellent brasses of the Assheton family are housed in the church as well as the armour of the last male heir, Sir Ralph, who died in 1765.

Middleton's other notable buildings include, Ye Olde Boar's Head, Alkrington Hall, Hopwood Hall, and Long Street Methodist Church, a fine example in *art nouveau* style of the work of local architect, Edgar Wood.

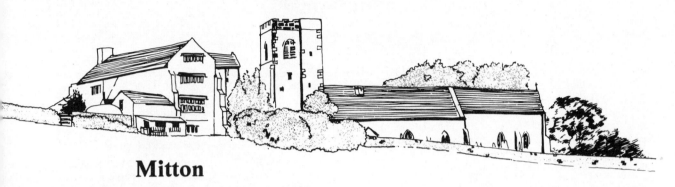

Mitton

The bank of the Ribble on which Mitton stands was, until 1974, in Yorkshire, yet throughout its history the links have been forged with Lancashire.

In 1594, Sir Richard Sherbourne of Stonyhurst decided to build his family's chapel in the twelfth century church of All Hallows. Here are many generations of the family — a unique history in stone, marble and alabaster.

The Ribble created problems for the travellers of old when journeying to the north or south. Romans, Normans, Border raiders, Ironsides, Kings and Queens, rich men and poor men, all had to cross the river, and this they did by ford, ferry, stepping stones and bridges. Many historically interesting crossings survive, none more so than here at Mitton where once a ferry crossed from the Mitton Boat Inn, now renamed the Aspinall's Arms. Today's traveller drives across a bridge built by Macadam when he constructed his 'new' turnpike road.

On the hill stands Mitton Hall, where priests from Cockersand Abbey lived when they served the church.

The Shirebourne Arms, where sat the Courts Leet, was once called the Three Fishes, a name derived from the abbey stones above the door.

Across the river are the wooded grounds of Little Mitton Hall, once the home of the Cateralls.

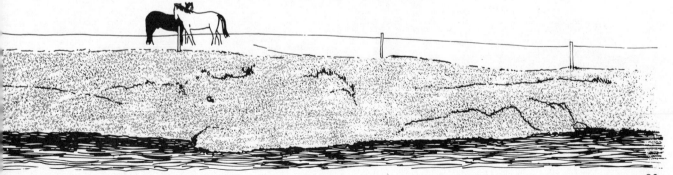

Newchurch-in-Pendle

At one time called Goldshaw Booth — until it gained its new church — the village clings close to the hill, the houses sheltering as best they can from the biting east winds.

Its fame stems not only from the numerous occasions it has won the Best Kept Village Competition, but also from its association with the Pendle witches. The souvenirs in the corner shop may be the only witches seen here today but the carved 'Eye of God' on the church tower has witnessed many witches and wizards attending the church services.

In 1612, many were hanged for their foolishness in disliking their kinsmen or neighbours and for telling a few tales of witchcraft.

The stone marked 'Alice Nutter' in the churchyard is reputed to be a witch's grave but whether it is or not is questionable.

There is no choice in Newchurch, you either go up hill or down. Up to Barley, down to Roughlee.

Pendle Hill dominates the area and acts as a focal point for many walkers, among whom was George Fox, founder of the Quaker movement.

Newton

Newton stands on the borders of the Royal Forest of Bowland. It is a quiet and beautiful village that once trembled to the sound of Roman Legions marching to and from the wall, fording the river below where the bridge now stands.

Later, the forest highway from Wigglesworth to Dunslop and Lancaster was routed through the village. How many people, one wonders, must have passed this way through the years?

Forest laws were strict. Even when large tracts of land were leased for farming and most of the game had vanished, villagers had still to be cautious when considering poaching, felling trees, fishing in rivers, owning dogs capable of catching deer, or trespassing to cut rushes for thatch.

One of George Fox's followers came this way and, in 1767, founded a Meeting House for Friends, with a tiny sepulchre nearby. To start a school for Quaker children and 'poor children not being Quakers', John Brabbin left 20 guineas. 30 boarders and 6 village lads could be accommodated. To this school was sent a timid boy by the name of John Bright, the later orator and statesman. John and his fellow pupils could actually enjoy school — a unique condition in those days — interspersing lessons with fishing and learning to swim in the Hodder, and making expeditions to local lead mines and caves.

Ordsall Hall

An ancient gem set in Salford's dockland, Ordsall was first mentioned in a tax return of 1177, and it is probable that there was a house on the site by 1251, when David de Hulton held it as a manor.

In 1354, Sir John Radcliffe established his right to inherit the manor from Richard, the last of the de Hultons. It was Sir John who began building the present Hall. Its Star Chamber wing retains many original features, while the Great Hall, a smaller hall of the fourteenth century, was probably built in the 1520s, when Sir Alexander Radclyffe became High Sheriff of Lancashire.

The west wing, originally a separate building, was erected in 1639 by another Sir Alexander Radclyffe, who was already in financial difficulties when he was arrested for Royalist activities. His son, John, was forced to sell the Hall in 1662 to the Presbyterian, Colonel John Birch, so ending a 300 year connection between the Radclyffe family and Ordsall Hall.

The estate was owned successively by the Birches, the Oldfields, and the Stocks until 1756, when it was purchased by Samuel Hill of Shenstone. Two years later it was inherited by his nephew, Samuel Egerton.

Salford Corporation purchased Ordsall Hall in 1959 from the Executor of the Estate of Baron Egerton of Tatten.

Overton, Sunderland Point

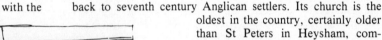

The only access by car to Sunderland Point is by car, with the road running across the beach. Be warned! because Sunderland is out of reach if the tide is mistimed.

Sunderland Point was an outer port for Lancaster in the eighteenth century, with a quay and warehouses built by a quaker, Robert Lawson. It is said that the first cotton-wool to be imported into England came in by way of Sunderland Point.

Overton's recorded history goes

back to seventh century Anglican settlers. Its church is the oldest in the country, certainly older than St Peters in Heysham, commanding excellent views across the Lune towards Glasson, and with a panorama of Pennines in the distance. The village centre with its white-walled houses wears well in the twentieth century, but it was once notorious for 'snatch 'ems', when many a drunken lad became an unwilling member of the Navy.

Piel Castle

Raids by marauding Scots motivated the building of Piel Castle on Foudrey by the Abbot of Furness, replacing an earlier stronghold erected in the reign of King Stephen. In addition, the abbot built a tower above the ancient town of Dalton, and provided a beacon on the hill beside the abbey.

Piel Castle served well, providing a safe anchorage for ships loading produce and iron ore (in which the area is rich) for foreign ports.

Access to Piel Island is by the long Causeway, that once carried the railway to Rea Island — where Trinity House pilots serving ships to and from Barrow had their station — and thence by ferry to Piel itself. Another way is to follow the example of the many weekenders who sail their own boats from the mainland.

A further attraction on the island is a pub called The Ship, where, for over a hundred years, a reputation has been maintained for hospitality and Nordic horseplay, with its *Knights of Piel,* and all that!

The year 1487 saw visitors with a more serious mission. An expeditionary force from Ireland landed with the intention of deposing Henry VII in favour of Lambert Simnel, son of an Oxford tradesman. Simnel was declared to be the Earl of Warwick and the rightful heir to the English throne. The march south by Simnel and his supporters met with total defeat.

Pilling

'All roads lead to Pilling', at least, while driving round the Flyde all the signposts appear to point that way.

Pilling, on the road to Cockersand Abbey, is an old village set amongst the marshes, safe from the sea these days, thanks to the vast drainage schemes which have made the Flyde the market garden of the north.

The village is set out on both banks of the river, each with a character of its own and both equally fascinating. It can boast two churches, one of which is Georgian, whose tall spire can be seen for miles. In the days when shipwrecks were an industry —

not that any were actually wrecked deliberately — the legendary Parson Potter was as keen as anyone to get to the shore.

Pilling has several claims to fame. The windmill, now a private house, ground the corn from the local farms; 'Pilling Moss', the salt washed turf used for lawns; and Pilling chickens have graced many a Lancashire table.

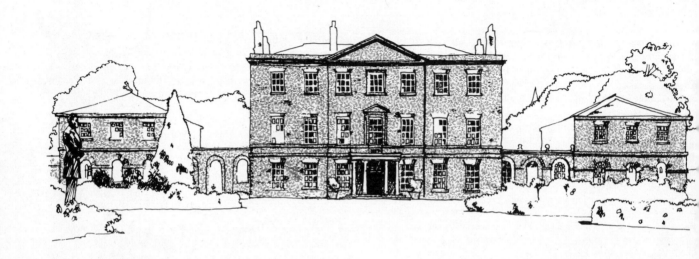

Platt Hall

Little is known about the early history of Platt Hall other than a twelfth century reference that makes clear it was then owned by the military religious Order of the Knights of St John. Later the ownership passed to the Platt family, with whom it remained until 1625, when it became the home of the Worsleys until 1907.

Charles Worsley was one of Cromwell's major-generals in the period of the Commonwealth.

The red brick house, built for John and Deborah Carhill-Worsley in 1764, is one of the few surviving eighteenth century buildings in Manchester. Of particular interest is the elegant

entrance hall and staircase, and the decorated first floor dining room.

By 1907, urban Manchester had sprawled out, consuming villages such as Rusholme. It was then that the Worsleys sold Platt Hall and the estate to the Manchester Corporation.

The grounds have been turned into a public park and the Hall now houses the internationally famous Gallery of English Costume, displaying the changing styles of everyday clothes and accessories of the past 350 years.

Outside there is a statue of Abraham Lincoln that commemorates a strike in the American Civil War.

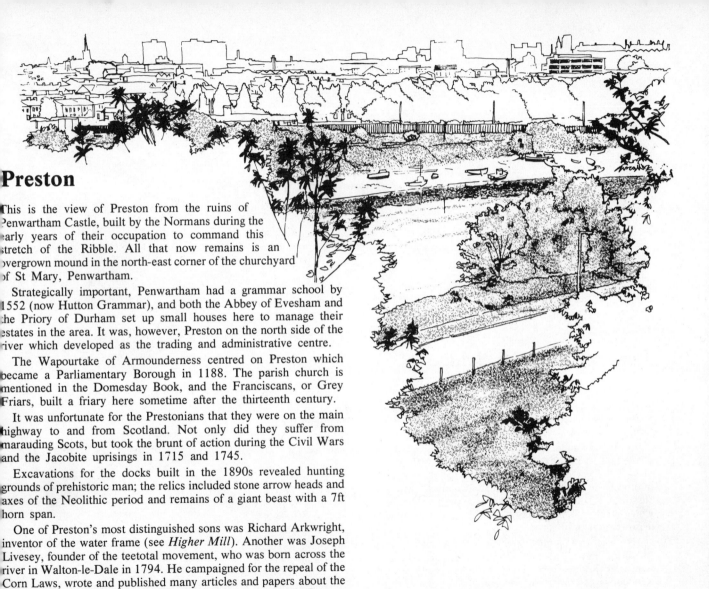

Preston

This is the view of Preston from the ruins of Penwartham Castle, built by the Normans during the early years of their occupation to command this stretch of the Ribble. All that now remains is an overgrown mound in the north-east corner of the churchyard of St Mary, Penwartham.

Strategically important, Penwartham had a grammar school by 1552 (now Hutton Grammar), and both the Abbey of Evesham and the Priory of Durham set up small houses here to manage their estates in the area. It was, however, Preston on the north side of the river which developed as the trading and administrative centre.

The Wapourtake of Armounderness centred on Preston which became a Parliamentary Borough in 1188. The parish church is mentioned in the Domesday Book, and the Franciscans, or Grey Friars, built a friary here sometime after the thirteenth century.

It was unfortunate for the Prestonians that they were on the main highway to and from Scotland. Not only did they suffer from marauding Scots, but took the brunt of action during the Civil Wars and the Jacobite uprisings in 1715 and 1745.

Excavations for the docks built in the 1890s revealed hunting grounds of prehistoric man; the relics included stone arrow heads and axes of the Neolithic period and remains of a giant beast with a 7ft horn span.

One of Preston's most distinguished sons was Richard Arkwright, inventor of the water frame (see *Higher Mill*). Another was Joseph Livesey, founder of the teetotal movement, who was born across the river in Walton-le-Dale in 1794. He campaigned for the repeal of the Corn Laws, wrote and published many articles and papers about the plight of the poor and, on 15 January 1844, founded the *Preston Guardian*.

91

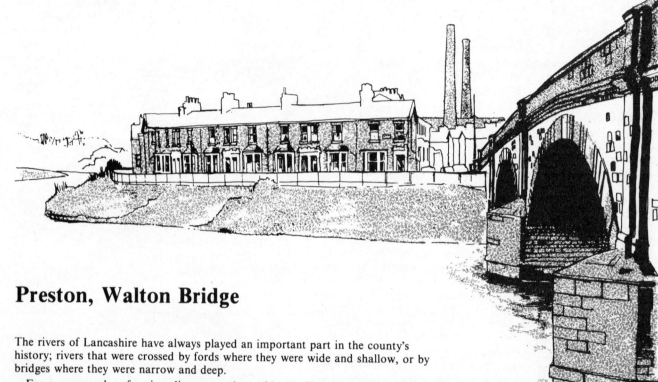

Preston, Walton Bridge

The rivers of Lancashire have always played an important part in the county's history; rivers that were crossed by fords where they were wide and shallow, or by bridges where they were narrow and deep.

For a commander of an invading army, the rapid and efficient crossing of rivers is of the highest priority. For those who are threatened, the rivers provide the natural lines of defence, and a view across the Ribble was, for many marauding Scots, the limit to their incursion into England. In 1648, during the Second Civil War, Hamilton's 24,000 strong army was out-manoeuvered by Cromwell at Walton Bridge which resulted in a running battle all the way to Warrington Bridge, where 4,000 men were taken prisoner.

The Scottish Jacobites fared no better when, at the invitation of the Lancashire Jacobites, they invaded England in 1715. James Edward was proclaimed king in Lancaster on the 7th November and the invaders marched on to Preston, where they were converged on by the two Hanoverian armies under Generals Wills and Carpenter, and forced to surrender on the 13th November.

Radcliffe Tower

In 1066 Radcliffe belonged to Edward the Confesser. Later, a conquesting Norman Knight was given the estate and took the name for his own — Radcliffe, meaning a 'cliff of red sandstone'. It was to be the family seat for over 500 years.

The Radcliffes of Radcliffe Tower became one of the most powerful and influential families in the country through the simple yet difficult ploy of marrying well and passing on the land to their descendants, resulting in the acquisition of the estates of Ordsall, Wythenshawe, Sunthills and many others.

The tower was built for defence, because of its position in the centre of a bend in the River Irwell. Dating from about 1403, the stone tower had connected to it what must have been a very impressive timber-framed Great Hall.

The Radcliffes were prominent at Tudor Courts. Robert Radcliffe, Lord Fitz Walter, was created Viscount Fitz Walter and Earl of Sussex in 1524. The third earl died without surviving issue in 1583.

In 1561 Radcliffe was sold to Richard Assheton of Middleton, the estate at that time including four water mills, a fulling mill, and four dovecotes.

When Sir Ralph Assheton died, his estates were divided between his two daughters, the manor of Radcliffe passing to Eleanor who married Sir Thomas Edgerton.

By the 1830s the Tower and Great Hall were in a ruinous state and were used by a farmer as a hayloft and cowshed.

Legend has it that the Tower was the scene for Percy's *Reliques* ballad *Lady Isabel's Tragedy or The Stepmother's Cruelty.* It tells the story of Sir James Radcliffe's only daughter who was killed by the cook under instructions from her stepmother. She was then baked and served in a pie to Sir James. A scullion boy revealed the truth and Sir James had the cook boiled in oil and his wife burnt at the stake.

Nearby stands the Church of St Bartholomew parts of which are thought to date from the twelfth century, though rebuilding and alterations were carried out in the nineteenth century.

Rawcliffe Hall

Herveus Walter arrived in England with William the Conqueror, and was rewarded for his efforts with lands at Warrington, Bewsey, Rawcliffe and Layton. The family name was later changed to Butler after one, Theobald, had been appointed Butler of Ireland.

In the mid-sixteenth century the family disposed of Layton Manor (modern Blackpool) and concentrated on Rawcliffe. Like many Lancashire families, the Butlers were strict Catholics, Royalists and Jacobites. Cardinal Allan is thought to have stayed in hiding here (see *Fleetwood).*

The Jacobite rebellion of 1715 was the beginning of the end for the Butlers. Squire Henry fled to France with the Young Pretender, later to return to the Isle of Man where he died. His son Richard was captured and sentenced to death, but he died the night before his execution. The lands were forfeited and, in 1723, sold to the Vicar of St Michael's and three others.

Today, the hall is the centre of a very popular country club and caravan club. It is a gabled house of many periods; half-timbered and rough-cast, with seventeenth century brick and nineteenth century improvements.

Ribchester

Set in the middle of the Ribble valley between Longridge Fell to the north and the moors to the south, the fort of Bremetennacum must have been a welcome sight to the marching armies of the great Roman Empire, on their way north to the wall.

There appears to have been two forts on the site. The first, quickly constructed in wood with earth defences, presumably with the role of supporting fortification to aid the advancing armies in the north. Rebuilding took place in the late 2nd century, about the same time as the modernisation of Corbridge, Chesterholme and Hardknott. This second fort was of a more permanent nature, with the outer walls, gateways and principle buildings fashioned in stone.

Two formations of auxiliary cavalry that are known to have been at Bremetennacum are the Asturian Cavalry, recruited in northern Spain, and the Sarmatians, who originated from the other side of the Roman Empire.

Sometime after the rebuilding the inter-ditches were filled in and new ditches dug further away from the fort, presumably to keep an enemy at optimum distance and allowing the use of *ballistae* — the Roman stone-throwing catapults.

Ribchester, White Bull Inn

A change in the path of the river cut through the ancient fort and destroyed much of what remained, but in so doing many archaeological treasures were uncovered. In 1796, the famous parade helmet was found on the river bank.

The river caused no more damage than the early settlers and obviously many of the buildings have been built with the stone from the fort, the approximate centre of which is marked by the church with its twelfth century nave and thirteenth century chancel. The pillars at the entrance of the White Bull Inn are examples of the re-use of stone. As a village, Ribchester is a delight of Georgian architecture and is always in contention in the Best Kept Village Competition.

Across the river can be seen Osbaldeston Hall amongst the trees. The Ribble is always busy with people fishing or messing about in canoes and boats. It has also brought invaders; the Romans are thought to have sailed up the river, mooring their boats at Anchor Hill. Irish pirates also came this way, as did the Celts in their coracles, but it was the Picts and the Scots who burnt down the fort. Today's invaders have to content themselves with viewing the museum and granaries.

Rivington

A central moorland community on the west side of Winter Hill, this quiet village must have been here long before recorded history. The nearby moors have ancient tumuli.

The local Pilkington family built the church and Bishop Pilkington founded the grammar school in 1568. The Unitarian Chapel dates from 1703 and is a gem. A short distance from the village are two great barns which are thought to have been built over a thousand years ago.

In 1724, a certain Mr Andrews, a man with an appreciation for a good view, built the Tower on the Pike, so that those venturing to the top of the Pike could ascend the Tower for an even finer prospect.

The valley was chosen for a reservoir by the Liverpool Corporation and in flooding the valley, the Hall, farms, and much of the village have gone. On the bank of the reservoir stands a replica of Liverpool Castle, built by the masons of Lord Leverhulme, the soap magnate.

Rochdale, Pioneers

It was a black era in the early 1800's, in the days before the repeal of the Corn Laws (see *Wigan* and *Calderdale*). But poverty brought a new spirit of self-help. Trading co-operatives were started in various parts of the country during the 1820s and '30s, loosely based on the philosophy of Robert Owen.

With the establishment of the Chartist Movement things began to move fast; nowhere more determinedly than in Rochdale. At a Chartist meeting, following a disasterous strike by Rochdale flannel weavers, it was suggested by Charles Howarth that a trading co-operative should be started in Rochdale.

Twenty-eight subscribers putting in 2d (less than 1p) saved £1 each. For £10 they rented a building in Toad Lane, once occupied by the Pioneer Regiment, and spent their remaining monies (£6.11s 1d) on stock. The opening was just before Christmas 1844.

These early Pioneers were subjected to much ridicule and scorn, but they worked on and flourished. Their ground rules were set out by Howarth and Daly; rules of which Robert Southey is quoted, 'a sprig of Owenism grafted upon a stack of common sense'.

The founding fathers had many other operations which sound appropriate even today: housing, education, manufactories, and cultural activities.

Roughlee Hall

The Royal Forest of Pendle, isolated as it was for many centuries, was just the place to harbour talk of devil worship, witchcraft and covens. Poor, simple souls indulged in strange rites; they probably took drugs, and believed they had done and seen strange things. Superstitious neighbours, intimidated and terrorised, were easily blackmailed.

'The devil's chief agent', Elizabeth Southernes, known as 'Old Mother Demdike', and her family became bitter rivals of Old Chattex (Anne Whittle) and her relatives. In 1612, both clans confessed, or perhaps boasted, their way to the gallows on Lancaster Moor. But Old Mother Demdike herself by then in her nineties, died in the dungeons of Lancaster Castle before the trial could take place.

Somehow, the others dragged Alice Nutter, the Mistress of Roughlee Hall, with them to the gibbet. She was accused of being involved with Old Mother Demdike in the killing of one, Henry Mitton and, despite her denials, was found guilty. Why her influential friends remained silent, or whether she dabbled in the black arts, are questions unanswered to this day.

Another witch hunt in 1633 produced a further collection of poor wretches, of whom 17 were found guilty on the strength of evidence of an 11-year-old boy. This time an enlightened judge sent several to London, and later most were reprieved.

Rufford Old Hall

During the reign of Henry II, the manor of Rufford was held by the Fyttons and in the thirteenth century it passed, through marriage, to the Hesketh family with whom it remained for almost seven hundred years. The original manor house probably stood about a mile to the north of the Old Hall, where a site is marked by an ancient moat.

The Old Hall, now in the care of the National Trust, was built on a bank of the river Douglas during the fifteenth century. At sometime in its history the west wing was destroyed, and the east wing was reconstructed in 1662. The

latter was again partly rebuilt in 1821. However, the Great Hall is quite undamaged and contains a magnificent movable screen.

The New Hall, now a hospital, was built in 1760 and stands in a park a short distance to the west.

The men of the Hesketh family were distinguished in war, both against the French and the Scots. However, plotting against Elizabeth I brought death to one. Lord Rufford was more fortunate in the Civil Wars; being over 80 years of age saved him from Cromwell's keen attentions.

A certain William Shakeshaft is recorded as being a member of the Hesketh Players. Could he have been, in reality, William Shakespeare in the vague and unaccounted years of his youth?

Samlesbury Church

Samlesbury Church lies to the right of the highway as the M62 drops into the Bibble Valley towards Preston.

Standing near the ford on the old route to Scotland, it was too tempting for the raiding Scots in the year 1322. They looted the church, laid waste the valley and fired Gospatrick's Hall. The owner, the Lord of Samlesbury, decided it would be more prudent to rebuild his Hall in the woods some distance away, renaming it Samlesbury Hall.

Samlesbury had more than its share of 'witches' in the witch hunts of 1616. However, they were acquitted when it was discovered that the main prosecution witness, a teenage girl by the name of Grace Sowerbutts and prone to fits, had been well coached in the false evidence on which the accusations had been based.

The church, with calf box pews dating from the seventeenth and eighteenth centuries, has its own witch's grave. She is said to have cracked the stone slab in her attempts to get out and haunt her husband, so iron bars were riveted to the stone. The cracks and rivet holes can still be seen.

On 15 May 1840, workmen excavating the nearby river's edge discovered a leaden chest containing silver coins, all struck prior to the year AD 928, ingots, ornaments and armlets; a treasure that has come to be known as the Cuerdale Hoard.

Samlesbury Hall

This Hall has all the ingredients of the popular conception of an ancient house, Black and white magpie timbers, ghosts, secret rooms and hides.

Originally called Gospatrick's Hall and built near Samlesbury Church, it was fired and the church looted by Robert the Bruce and his men in 1322.

Gilbert de Southworth decided to rebuild his Hall deep in the nearby woodland. To this nucleus of the Great Hall was added the domestic chapel by Sir Thomas Southworth in 1420, who also appended the south west wing, minstrels' gallery and fine oriel, as well as the glazing of the windows.

The Southworths and their men fought at Harfleur and Agincourt, and an archery field close to the Hall is believed to have been in use since that time.

The period after the Reformation was an extremely dangerous one for the staunch Catholic family of Southworth who constructed secret rooms to harbour priests and hold mass. Perhaps a few stories about ghosts and a 'white lady' were means of covering up the comings and goings of itinerant priests. True or not, the stories survive to this day.

John Southworth, a priest who cared for the poor in London, was arrested and executed. He was canonised in 1970.

Samlesbury Hall was sold in 1678 to the Braddyll family who took some of the carvings and part of the minstrels' gallery to Conishead Priory.

Sawley Abbey

In 1147, Abbot Benedict led a band of 12 brothers and 12 converts from Fountains Abbey to this sheltered spot by the Ribble, choosing it as the site for their new abbey.

For years they worked on the land and sheep pasture granted to them by the local gentry around Ingleborough and In Craven, and in the building of their great abbey. The enterprise involved the building of a cornmill, necessitating the diversion of a stream from the river to power it. The winters were cold and the site damp. Many of the monks suffered with rheums and ague, and pleaded to return to Fountains. But they had to stay.

The abbey lasted for nearly 400 years, the last abbot being one, Trafford, who took part in the Pilgrimage of Grace in protest to Henry VIII, and was later hanged for treason.

When dissolved by the monarch, the land and abbey buildings were sold; masonry, dress stones and roofing lead finding ready buyers.

Today, vistors are left with only rubble core to inspire the imagination, but there are some interesting tombstones and several carved flagstones, one bearing the profile of a sword.

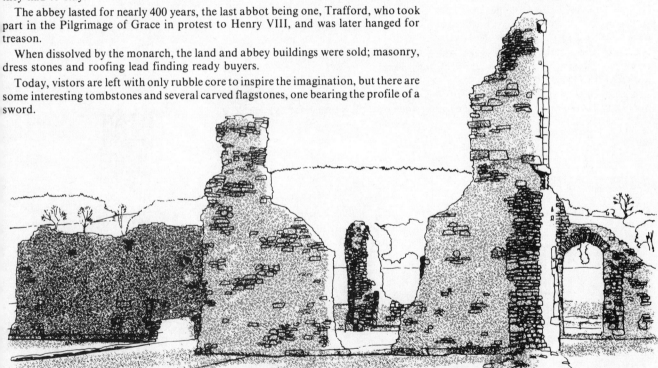

Scarisbrick Hall

Dating from 1180, this ancient home of the Scarisbrick family was, for centuries, surrounded by moss and mere.

The Scarisbricks were jovial, sporting, fun loving squires, who survived rebellions, and religious and political upheavals. Like many Lancashire families, they were Catholics who kept to their beliefs, harbouring priests in this seven-gabled timber and plaster house.

In 1814, Foster of Liverpool was commissioned by Thomas Scarisbrick to rebuild the Hall in the Gothic style. Thomas died in 1833 and his eccentric brother, Charles, with Augustus Welby Pugin gave the Hall an even more outrageous Gothic appearance, making annual sorties into Europe in search of treasures to adorn the house.

Charles was succeeded by his sister, Anne, who was at least equally eccentric! Anne employed Pugin's son and, between them, they doubled the height of the tower and increased the elaboration of the Hall.

After passing to the Marquis de Casteja, Scarisbrick Hall was eventually auctioned. In the 1950s the Hall was a teacher training college and now, still with an educational role, it is a private school.

Sefton

Although perilously close on the outskirts of Liverpool, the fourteenth century spire of the Church of St Helen can be seen for miles across the low farmland. It is to be hoped the steel shutters on the windows and doors will repel troublemakers, for the church contains many fine wood carvings, brasses and monuments, including a mailed effigy stemming from 1296.

Frequently bitter rivals in their lifetimes, the families of the Blundells and the Molyneux lie here in peace; old campaigners from the Crusades, Crecy, Agincourt and Flodden; supporters of the Stewart and Jacobite causes; Royalists through and through.

The Moylneux family home stood here on the bank of the Alt, until they moved to Croxteth. The old hall was demolished in 1720.

At a parish meeting held in the church in the late eighteenth century, it was decided to regulate the Alt, thereby safeguarding some 5,000 acres of land from being flooded for half the year. The good work started then is still maintained today.

There has been a water-driven cornmill beside the Alt since the 1590s.

Slaidburn

Slaidburn and Newton were 'vils' set in the Royal Forest of Bowland; a forest or 'foris' without trees, where Saxons and Normans alike engaged in the royal sport of hunting. Most of the forest was in Yorkshire but was still part of the Lancashire Dukedom, so it was no surprise when it became part of new Lancashire in 1974.

Forest laws were keen, with Halmote Courts (the courts of common law) held at Waddington and Slaidburn. One court-room was at Slaidburn's inn that is now known as the 'Hark to Bounty'.

Slaidburn is a haunt of artists, revelling in its hodder sidewalks, the green, cobble-edged streets and fascinating cottages.

St Andrews, the ancient church with its seventeenth century box pews and Jacobean three-decker pulpit, stands on the edge of the village, next to what must be the most elegant primary school in the country, founded as a grammar school in 1717.

Smithill's Hall

With a chapel consecrated in 1793, this place is reputed by legend to have been where the Saxon kings held court.

From the twelfth century, the lands were held by the Knights Hospitallers of St John of Jerusalem, later passing to the Radcliffe family of Radcliffe and Ordsall. In early Tudor times the estate was bought by the Bartons, followed by the Byroms in 1723 and the Ainsworths in 1801. The present owners are the Bolton Corporation, who purchased Smithill's Hall in 1933.

The Great Hall and adjoining wing date back to the fourteenth century. About the year 1516, Andrew Barton made several improvements, adding a withdrawing room and re-building the chapel.

It was Andrew's son, Roger Barton, who had the protestant Vicar of Deane, George Marsh, brought to the Upper Green Chamber to be examined, during which he was subjected to much taunting and abuse, and was finally charged with heresy. It is said that, outraged by the injustice, he stamped his foot as he left the Chamber; the 'bloody footprint' can be seen today! The unfortunate vicar was taken to Chester where he suffered death by burning.

Today part of the Hall is a home for the elderly. There are nature trails in the grounds, as well as a restaurant and a garden centre.

Southport

Lancashire is justly famous for its seaside resorts. Each has its own character and attracts its own type of visitor. The best known is Blackpool with its tower and Golden Mile, but Southport's charm is in that it has retained much of its earlier architecture.

Nearby Churchtown was once the most important place on the shore, with its ancient church (rebuilt in the 1730s) and its grammar school. The sudden popularity of sea bathing in the eighteenth century and the resulting flow of visitors prompted an innkeeper by the name of Sutton to erect, first a bathing hut, a refreshment kiosk, and then to build the hotel, which gained the name 'Southport'.

In 1803 William, Duke of Gloucester, Commander of the North West Approaches, waited here for the French invasion that never came. His time was spent engaged in bathing. A Frenchman came later, in 1815, when Louis Philippe, the future king of France, also enjoyed himself here. Preludes of Southport's Victorian popularity.

Disaster threatened in the 1860s when the sea began to recede. To counter this a pier was built and, in the 1880s, the marine lake and gardens were laid out.

Today, a walk down Lord Street is to see and enjoy the very best in Victorian splendour.

Speke Hall

Situated eight miles from Liverpool, on the banks of the Mersey, now with the airport as its neighbour, the manor of Speke is recorded in the Domesday Book as being held by one, Octred, from about 1066. The present Speke Hall was built between 1490 and 1612, on a site adjacent to the original building. It is a particularly fine example of a Tudor half-timbered manor house, and illustrates well the changing influences of the Gothic, Renaissance and Flemish styles.

In south Lancashire and Cheshire, stone was difficult to quarry, whilst wood was plentiful, which is why the area is rich in black and white medieval and Tudor buildings.

Speke was the medieval home of the Norrises and held by them until 1700.

By 1585, it was treasonable to hold mass, to be a Roman Catholic priest, or to harbour one. The Norrises remained faithful to the Church of Rome and, because they resisted the Reformation, had heavy fines imposed on them. The chapel and priest holes in and by the side of the chimney stacks are relics of this period.

During the Civil War the Norris family fought on the side of the King, resulting in further financial loss, including the penalty of having to supply timber for the rebuilding of Liverpool, following successive sieges.

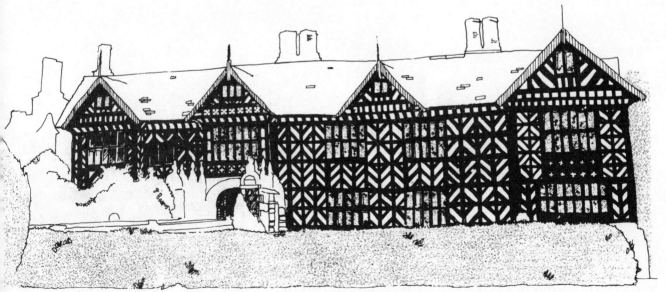

Stoneyhurst College

Stoneyhurst Hall, as it was originally known, was the home of the Sherburnes who came here in the sixteenth century from nearby Bailey Hall.

The Sherburnes' home was built on the site of an earlier house and the building took several generations of the family, the work starting with the first of four Richard Sherburnes.

When Cromwell stayed here, as an unwelcome guest in 1648 the building was still unfinished. (See *Hodder Bridge).* The third and fourth of the Richard Sherburnes were unable to contribute much to the building; in fact the fourth Richard died in Manchester Jail because of his loyalty to James II and the Jacobite cause.

It was Nicholas Sherburne who, after marrying a wealthy heiress, was able to complete the Hall. His son died suddenly while still a child and the estate passed through the female line to the Wells family.

When the Jesuits were evicted from their school at St Omar following the French Revolution, they were offered Stoneyhurst Hall, which was by then deserted, as a temporary residence. They arrived on 29 August 1794 and the school has flourished since. Many improvements have been made; the church was built in 1835, followed by the observatory in 1838.

Swarthmoor Hall

Lancashire was, in many ways, isolated from the main stream of church and religious life. It was therefore a rich and fertile ground for those wishing to sow non-conformist ideals and beliefs and, by the time George Fox was on the road preaching and writing his 'journal', there were many 'seekers' eager to listen. One such person was Margaret Fell, wife of the influential magistrate, Thomas Fell, and mother of their eight children.

The Fells lived at Swarthmoor Hall and, in June 1652, George Fox made his fateful visit when he convinced Margaret her family and many of the household as to the 'truth' seen by him and his followers.

Judge Fell was away on circuit at the time and an important meeting between him and George Fox had to be arranged later, after which regular Sunday meetings were held in the Great Hall for 38 years.

Swarthmore Hall became the headquarters of the Quaker Movement and Margaret Fell became the Mother of Quakerism, with help from her daughters who all married Quakers.

In 1660 Margaret Fell visited London to persuade Charles II to keep his promise of religious toleration. Later, 4,000 Quakers were freed from prison. But Margaret found herself in Lancashire Jail in 1664 and was not released until 1668, when granted a free pardon from the king. In the following year she was married to George Fox. She is buried at Sunbrick Sepulchre (see *Birkrigg*).

Thornton, Marsh Mill

This land, now known as the *fylde* (field) was once called Amounderness. In the sixteenth century there were not less than 40 'peg' or 'post' windmills on this land sometimes called Amounderness and Windmill Land. Except for one 'post' at Wharton, all have perished before the weather. The early mills were replaced by sturdier brick 'tower' mills and several of these have been converted into private residences.

The best preserved windmill in the county is Marsh Mill, built in 1794 by Ralph Slater who was also responsible for the construction of other mills at Pilling and Clifton.

112

Marsh Mill was originally used to grind corn but from the end of the last century until 1922 its function was to grind meal for farm animals, after being outdated by modern equipment producing finer white flour.

Until 1962 the mill had Cubitt's Patent Sails, two of which were lost in a gale and the other two removed for safety. The present sails, of a type carried when the mill was first built, each has a radius or *whip* of 30ft. Up to 60 horse power could be achieved to turn the four 4ft diameter stones.

The mill is topped by a distinctive boat-shaped cap, once a common sight in the north-west, probably fashioned by local boat-builders.

Towneley Hall

Built originally as a hunting lodge, Towneley Hall was extended into a Tudor mansion and, later, altered to meet Georgian tastes. Sir Richard de Towneley, Sheriff of the county, and the first of the family to be installed with knighthood, had a grandson who fought at Agincourt.

The Towneleys were a Catholic family, whose devotion, at the time of the Reformation, was split between crown and church. John Towneley sheltered priests and had mass said in secret; for this he was imprisoned in 1564 and not released until 1601, at the age of 73.

The family's faith and following caused a turbulent history. Charles Towneley supported Charles I and died at the Battle of Marston Moor. His son, Richard, had to flee the country to avoid arrest for his part in the attempt to restore James II to the throne; his grandson, also Richard, joined the 1715 Jacobite rebellion, was captured but later acquitted. His less fortunate brother, who took part in the 1745 uprising, with the Manchester Regiment, was executed after the fall of Carlisle. Another member of the family forced to flee the country was Sir John, after the Battle of Culloden.

Peregrine Edward Towneley, like his ancestor, Sir Richard, was installed High Sheriff of Lancashire in 1828.

Alice Many Towneley (Lady O'Hagan) donated to the Burnley Corporation in 1901, the Hall with its impressive collection of paintings, handmade glass, furniture, vestments, plasterwork and priestholes.

Turton Stone Circle

To the north west of Turton Tower are the hills known as Turton Heights, with the summit marked by a trig stone. Some yards to the north west stand the remains of what is said to be a Druid's stone circle — only 51ft 6ins in diameter — and the two or three stones that remain are small. The 'hele' is now marked with a cross.

The Rev T. Boston Johnstone, in his book *Religious History of Bolton*, published in 1887, describes the circle as seen on a visit here in 1850. There were then six stones standing, varying in height from 1ft to 4ft 5ins. After a subsequent  visit some years later he reported that the circle had suffered considerable damage, several of the larger stones having been smashed.

To the southwest there is evidence of a larger circle of about 72ft diameter. Within the circumference the grass is different from the moorland grass, suggesting there may have been cattle impounded here (see Birkrigg Common).

In the book, *Mysterious Lancashire*, P. Rickman and G. Nown explain, in some detail, Watkin's 'Ley System', with several drawings aligning the many *tumuli* in the Rivington/Belmont area, as well as possible connections between ancient churches, standing stones, wells and moats throughout the county.

Turton Tower

A fifteenth century stone pele tower which, over the years, had been added to, making it a fascinating example of expansion and maturity.

In the sixteenth century, the timbered south wing and hallway were added and the tower raised in height.

A stone frontage was built on the cottage wing during a period of nineteenth century restoration; at the same time, the dining room was panelled with timber purchased and brought from Middleton Hall, Manchester. In 1628 the estate was bought by Humphrey Chetham of Clayton Hall in Droylsdon.

Although a staunch Parliamentarian, he was offered a knighthood by Charles I but refused to accept the accolade, and was fined in consequence. However, he could not refuse the office of High Sheriff and had the onerous duty of collecting King Charles' 'Ship Money'. When the Civil War broke out in 1642, Humphrey Chetham was naturally on the side of the Roundheads and was appointed Treasurer for the cause in Lancashire; Turton Tower being used for quartering Roundhead troops.

The estate remained in the Chetham family until 1835, when it passed to a local man, James Kay. It was sold to the Knowles family in 1890 and, forty years later, was passed to the local authority.

Ulverston

On Head Hill, high above the ancient town, stands a memorial to Ulverston's most famous son, John Barrow, born here in 1764 and a student at the Town Bank Grammar School. It is no accident that the memorial takes the form of the third Eddystone lighthouse; Barrow worked with John Smeaton, the designer of the real thing.

John Barrow's early interests were astronomy and mathematics which served him well through a varied career, encompassing voyages to the whaling grounds of Greenland, teaching at Greenwich, and surveying the Cape of Good Hope. He was also sometime controller of the Embassy Household in China, and wrote accounts for the prime minister, William Pitt. He became Secretary to the Admiralty (a post once held by Samuel Pepys), after returning from an Arctic expedition. He even found time to be a founder member of the Royal Geographic Society.

Not only was the lighthouse erected to his memory, but Cape Barrow, Point Barrow and the Barrow Straights, bear his name.

On the days when the flag flies, those who have the mind and the energy can climb Hoad Hill and the steps inside the lighthouse, perhaps to watch the sunset over Low Furness, from Barrow to Cartmel, with Conishead twinkling through the trees, contrasting with the quiet majestic heart of the Lakes to the north.

Below are the chimneys and rooftops of Ulverston, whose highways have witnessed the comings and goings of armies, royal convoys, and those passing through on Abbey business, since its charter was granted by Edward I.

George Fox came this way in June 1652, stopping at Swarthmoor Hall for the fateful meeting with Margaret and Judge Fell. When the judge died in 1688 he was buried by torchlight under his pew in Ulverston Parish Church. A benificiary of his will was a new school that was destined to be the Ulverston Grammar School.

Urswick

There is thought to have been a pagan site here before the church of St Mary and St Michael was built sometime between the years 827 and 927, as the perimeter walls of the churchyard scribe a rough circle. The nave and lower part of the tower are probably pre-Norman, with the chancel added about the year 1200.

On the first roof beam is carved '1598. W.L.V.', the letters standing for William Lindow, Vicar, and the date is when the steeper thatched roof was replaced.

In the chancel are some interesting humorous woodcarvings, and the carvings on the altar rails, the vestry and main doors, the sides of the reredos, the rood screen, and the top of the font, are of equal note. The three-decker pulpit is of a type used in Georgian times.

Also to be seen are portions of a tenth century Viking cross, and late nineth century pre-Viking or Anglo-Saxon cross, whose runics tell that 'uneini set up is memorial to his son Torptred. Pray for his soul. Lyl wrought this'.

On the right hand wall of the porch can be seen the marks made when Tudor archers sharpened their arrows. By law, they had to practise archery each Sunday after the church service.

Warrington

The Romans came this way and built their fort at Wilderspool.

The parish church was dedicated to St Elfin, and at some time during or after the thirteenth century, the gospel-preaching Austin or Augustine Friars built their friary.

In 1495, the Earl of Derby paid for the rebuilding of the bridge in order that his stepson, King Henry, could visit him at Knowsley.

Warrington was a 'frontier town' on the fordable banks of the Mersey and, being placed midway between Liverpool and Manchester, it was a frequent stop-over and base for many warfaring armies (see *Haigh Hall*).

Doubtless the town's most spectacular period was during the Civil Wars, when it was taken and retaken. Two old buildings on opposite sides of the same street — one being the Marquess of Granby — have plaques on the walls which record the fact that both Oliver Cromwell, in command of the Parliamentary army, and the Earl of Dover, commanding the Royalist forces, had their headquarters nearby (see *Preston, Walton Bridge*). Cromwell's statue is situated near the bridge in front of what was the old Warrington Academy, which was established in 1757.

The skills and trades of the Warrington are many and varied, such as sail-making; iron-founding; pin, lock and tool-making; copper wire production; soap-making, and distilling.

The Manchester Ship Canal, opened in May 1844 by Queen Victoria, cuts it way through the south side of the town.

In the twentieth century, Warrington has become a New Town and a part of Cheshire. Being in the centre of the east-west, north-south motor complex, the town attracts industry from all over the world,

Warton

A village at the foot of the crag overlooking Morecambe Bay. On this crag the Celts built a fort and, centuries later, their descendants kept watch for distant beacons giving warning of marauding Scots, building thick-walled peles in defence.

As a boy, Matthew Hutton was given his first private lessons at Warton. Hutton became Bishop of Durham and, later, of York. Queen Elizabeth I granted him a charter to establish, in Warton, a grammar school and a hospital for six old men.

The local Washington family built the tower of St Oswald's church and it is said that the design formed the basis of the American flag. George Washington, the first American president, was directly descended from this family; on the 4th July each year 'Stars and Stripes' are flown from the church tower.

The ruins opposite the church are known as the Rectory. Built at the end of the thirteenth century by the de Thweng family, the building has remained uniquely unchanged over the years.

Whalley Abbey

In 1296, Henry de Lacy willed the parish of Whalley to the Cistercian monks of Stanlaw who came here after the death of their dean, Peter de Cestria. They organised and managed their new lands and started work on the abbey, the building of which continued until the fifteenth century.

Whalley became a hub of ecclesiastical affairs, with the coming and going of travellers on abbey business. Many of the travellers were sheltered at the abbey's west gatehouse, but the more noble among them found hospitality and entertainment at the abbot's table.

It was the abbey that instigated the building of a bridge over the river to replace a ford.

Whalley's last abbot was John Paslew, who was executed in 1537. With the Dissolution in 1537, much of the abbey was sold. The Southworths used abbey masonry for their family chapel and parlour windows at Samlesbury Hall, while a great deal of the facing stones were used for many of the local buildings. Fortunately, the finely carved canopied choir stalls were moved to the church.

The Asshetons converted the abbot's dwelling into their family home, but to have a full scale abbey in the garden was too much and, during the 1660s, most of it was levelled.

Whalley Church

Christianity came to Whalley early in the dark ages after the Roman occupation. The evangelist could have been St Augustine or, more likely, St Paulinus and his missionaries in 627, after the conversion of Northumbria.

Whoever the founder, there are more than one thousand years of devotion attached to this venerable building. Whalley's parish spread over 400 miles and became one of the wealthiest; at first under the direction of Lichfield and then Chester.

Three styles of crosses are to be found in the churchyard: Anglo-Celtic, Anglian and Anglo-Norse. Nothing remains of the ancient wooden church, though there are fragments of the first stone structure. The chancel is probably from the twelfth century; the nave was lengthened in the thirteenth and fourteenth centuries. In the mid-fifteenth century the belfrey tower was added and the nave roof raised, thus completing the building.

Whalley is a village that turned its back on the Industrial Revolution, with hand-loom weavers working here till quite late in the nineteenth century. The early textile factories which were built are to be found either up or down stream but not in the village itself.

The abbey Corn Mill was built within a 100yds or so of the abbey grounds on the site of an earlier mill, but since 1961 the water-wheel has been stilled.

Wigan

Lancashire was in a unique position during the industrial revolution; the consistent rainfall and fast-flowing Pennine streams powered the early water mills. With the development of steam power, Lancastrians found themselves standing on some of the richest coal deposits in Britain.

The ever-increasing demand for coal called for deeper mines, new methods of drainage, powered cutting, mechanised sating and cleaning, and cheap efficient transportation. Much of the design, development and production was done in the Lancashire coalfield.

It was the excessive cost of transporting coal and other raw minerals like rock salt, along with the development of the chemical industry, that pioneered turnpike roads, tramways, canals, and the railways. A stretch of original tramway at Winstay Hall was used by Robert Daglish for his experiments with a locomotive between 1812 and 1816.

Coalmining in the area between Wigan and Leigh was being carried on in Tudor and Stuart times. Even in those early mining days, deeds of land did not necessarily include mineral rights. Little remains of the very early mines, but 'Haigh Sough' — a drain — was started by Sir Roger Bradshaigh of Haigh between 1653 and 1670.

The industrial revolution is exciting in retrospect but the lot of the worker was a miserable one. Poverty, lock-outs, child labour and prostitution were simply everyday facts.

The revolutions which took place in America and France must have panicked many a politician and dignitary, as the Peterloo affair must illustrate well. The trade unions had a bloody birth.

Fredrick Engel's book *Conditions of the English Working Class 1844* vividly describes the back-street life in such places as Manchester, Salford and Stockport.

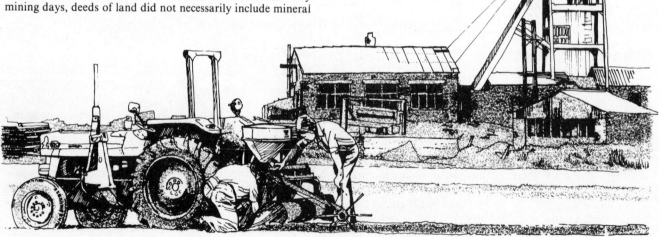

Worsley, Bridgewater Canal

The Bridgewater Canal was the second to be cut in England; the first, also in Lancashire, being the Sankey Navigation.

The Duke of Bridgewater, disenchanted with the social life of London, concerned himself with running his estates and coal mines. Finding it cost more to convey coal than to mine it, he looked for a cheaper means of transportation. He eventually decided to build a canal and enlisted the services of his estates agent, John Gilbert, and James Brindley, the eccentric but brilliant self-taught engineer.

Work started in 1759. A year later it was decided to re-route the canal at Monton and cross the river Irwell with an aquaduct at Barton; a spectacular piece of engineering. The canal was opened in 1761 and resulted in a reduction in the cost of coal at Manchester from 1 shilling to 4 pence a hundredweight.

Over the next 13 years this remarkable team went on to build over 365 miles of canals. The Duke also used underground canals to connect his colliery with the terminus at Worsley — a system of over 40 miles.

Canals were also used to transport passengers, with a daily service running from the steps of The Packetboat to Manchester.

Worsley's 'black and white' courthouse is Victorian, built by a relative of the old Duke, the first Earl of Ellesmere.

Wrea Green

A village on the north side of the Ribble, in that rich lush carpet of green farmland which is so important to Lancashire's economy.

The most outstanding feature of the village is its green. If there was a competition for the village which had the largest green, then Wrea Green would surely be one of the finalists. Until 1972 the lord of the manor could still claim the grazing rights of his livestock.

The green with its duckpond is surrounded by well balanced and beautifully kept houses, church, post office, store, and, down the lane, the railway station. The water tap carries a small plaque commemorating the winning of the Best Kept Village Competition. There is a farm on the far side of the village, and not far away the ruins of a tower windmill.

To the east of the village is Ribby Hall, built in the Georgian style in the 1820s for the Hornbys. It is now the permanent headquarters of the Royal Lancashire Agricultural Show.

Wray

A village settled by Norsemen, the word *wray* meaning an 'out of the way corner'. In some ways it still is, with cobbled lined streets and an architecture dating back to Tudor and Jacobean times. A sleepy village from the past perhaps, but also very much of today.

Wray lies where the Roeburn meets the Hindburn and, in August 1967, a raging flood changed the face of the village; ripping away bridges, walls, cottages and trees, though there are few reminders visible now.

This is a village where dalesman met shepherd; where, for a time, farming and industry developed side-by-side. Hundreds were employed in the mills along the banks of the Roeburn, spinning China silk or making tall silk hats. Gone now are the days when one could find here woodturners, nail makers, bobbin makers, wheel-wrights, and clog blockmakers.

Wray is a place where people are important. At the time of my visit I had the impression that the entire population from miles around had come to wish well to one of the local girls on her wedding day. In the main street, full of cars, the village lads were up to their usual mischief, while old ladies looked on with their own memories.

Wycoller

Set firmly in a dene east of Colne, this old village is the centrepiece of a new country park.

The fine Tudor Hall was the home of the Cunliffes, a family actively interested in the sports of hunting and cock fighting.

Once, it is said, the Hall was destroyed by a mad woman setting fire to it, and the ruins are believed to have inspired Charlotte Bronte to make Wycoller the Ferndean Hall of *Jane Eyre*. The Hall is reputed to be haunted and those who doubt it should perhaps make a visit here at dusk in mid-winter!

It was a village of the handloom weavers, with as many as 300 to 400 people producing cloth to be sold in the market at Colne. The Industrial Revolution brought an end to the

prosperity and the village, with the Hall, fell into ruin. Only the farmers stayed.

Thanks to the County Council, the Friends of Wycoller, a government grant and the creation of the country park, all is now alive with industry, and people are back in the village, restoring cottages and barns.

A shallow river runs through the centre of Wycoller, crossed by bridges and a ford. The most ancient bridges stand either side of the ford. One, a twin-arched bridge, dating from the fifteenth century, well demonstrates the problems faced by civil engineers. The other, a bridge made from stone slabs, is equally interesting and even older.

Wythenshawe Hall

The estate which dates back to 1316 became the home of the Tatton family in 1370, and here they stayed for over 500 years.

The original moated hall was rebuilt in the familiar black and white style during the reign of Henry VIII, and there were further additions during the Elizabethan, Jacobean and Georgian periods. Additional building during the nineteenth century destroyed the remains of the chapel.

Monuments to various members of the Tatton family are to be found in Northenden Church.

There are many legends about the hall, but what we know for a fact is that the Parliamentarians put it to siege during the Civil War, and Royalist Robert Tatton held out for what must have been a very long 18 months. Only when the hall had been reduced to a ruin around him — thanks to two large pieces of ordnance specially brought from Manchester — did he finally surrender.

The hall and surrounding parklands were bought from the Tatton family by the late Lord and Lady Simon of Wythenshawe, and presented by them in 1926 to the people of Manchester.

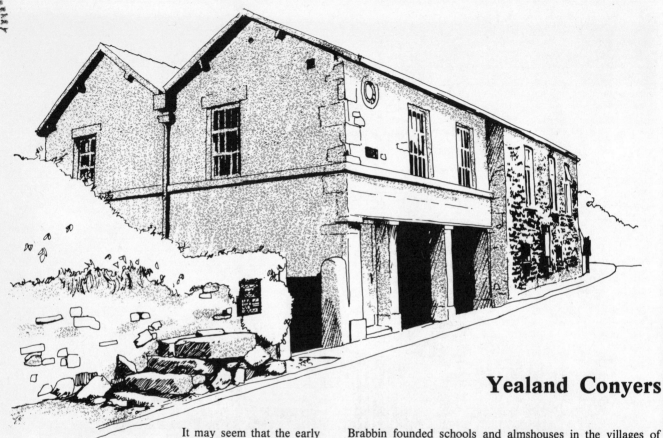

Yealand Conyers

It may seem that the early Quakers were narrow, strict and puritanical in outlook and behaviour. Such discipline helped them withstand the persecution and shocking conditions which they had to face. However, many individuals in the Quaker movement did much to improve the educational, social and financial situation of fellow Lancastrians. Many were business men engaged in the textile trade, such as the Jackson brothers of Caldervale and John Bright of Rochdale. John Brabbin founded schools and almshouses in the villages of Newton and Chipping.

Many Meeting Houses were established in rural areas, and that established in 1692 in Yealand Conyers is typical; the village being one of the most attractive in the county.

Other Meeting Houses in Lancashire include: Swarthmoor Hall (c1600), Swarthmoor Meeting House (1688), Colthouse (1688), Cawshawbooth (1715), St Helens (1678), and Lancaster (1708).